W9-BCT-936

Parliamentary Procedure

Parliamentary Procedure

Hugo E. Hellman

THE MACMILLAN COMPANY, *New York*
COLLIER-MACMILLAN LIMITED, *London*

Wingate College Library

© Copyright, Hugo E. Hellman, 1966

All rights reserved. No part of this book may be reproduced or utilized in any form or by any means, electronic or mechanical, including photocopying, recording or by an information storage and retrieval system, without permission in writing from the Publisher.

First Printing

Library of Congress catalog card number: 66–17900

THE MACMILLAN COMPANY, NEW YORK
COLLIER-MACMILLAN CANADA, LTD., TORONTO, ONTARIO

Printed in the United States of America

091840

To Dr. William M. Lamers, parliamentarian, author, poet, playwright, and teacher, who taught me all of the parliamentary procedure I know, and most of whatever else has proved worthwhile.

Tu se' lo mio maestro, e il mio autore;
tu se' solo colui, da cui io tolsi
lo bello stile, che m' ha fatto onore.

Foreword

IT IS MORE important to be able to use parliamentary rules than to recite them without understanding. Thus, instead of beginning with a list of rules to be memorized, this textbook, lesson by lesson, explains how a member uses parliamentary procedure in meetings. In this process the rules are learned so a member will participate in organizations with confidence and understanding.

The second section is directed to the chairman or presiding officer. Professor Hellman first explains the *art* of presiding: how to run a meeting smoothly and with dignity. Then he takes up the *science* of presiding: the use and interpretation of parliamentary procedure. Each rule is discussed from the point of view of the chairman. Especially helpful are four principles that answer perennial questions about the precedence of motions, amendments, debatability, and voting. The chart on the inside back cover gives additional aid to the chairman.

The concluding section gives instructions on forming organizations and exercises for practicing parliamentary procedure. For those who wish further study in the field, Professor Hellman includes a list of additional reference books.

An important underlying theme of this volume is that parliamentary rules enable an organization to approach agreement through democratic means. The rules are not a method of obtaining and enforcing majority opinion, but are devised to enable everyone to participate in initiating proposals and modifying or developing them, so that the best and most creative thinking goes into the final decision.

Dr. Hugo Hellman is the Director of the School of Speech and Professor of Speech at Marquette University. In writing this book he has utilized thirty years of experience in teaching parliamentary procedure. Nationally known as a parliamentarian, he serves as a consultant on parliamentary procedure for many national organizations.

Arthur C. Hastings
Stanford University

Contents

Parliamentary Procedure

PART I

Participating as a Member

PARLIAMENTARY Procedure may be defined as the way in which an organization will be governed and the order by which its meetings will be run if it agrees to follow Robert's Rules of Order. This book is intended to help you learn how to be an effective member of such organizations and how to participate effectively in their meetings.

The approach of this book is unique in that it is not a textbook of the rules. It is a textbook of the procedure. The approach is functional and practical. It explains how things are done. It tells you what you must do and how to do it if you would accomplish those things which, as a member, you may want to do.

The functional and practical approach is taken here for several reasons. The first is that it makes the task of learning the procedure a great deal easier. We need to learn only those rules which normally come into use in the affairs of the typical contemporary organizations to which you may expect to belong. In setting out to learn the procedure directly, as opposed to learning the body of rules, we can go directly and precisely to what we are seeking. This is analogous to learning to drive an automobile by taking a lesson behind the wheel and out on the street or highway, as opposed to an arm chair study of the traffic ordinances and statutes. In taking a driving lesson behind the wheel, you are taken through the experience of starting the engine, moving out forward, backing up, steering on the right side of the street, executing right and left turns and the many other things which you will want to do as an accomplished driver. In the following pages, this book takes you through the experiences involved in being an accomplished and effective member of an organized group. You learn how to present a piece of business, discuss it, modify it, postpone it, and so on. You learn how meetings are run and how you can protect your rights and privileges in them. You will not learn all of the Rules, but you will learn all of the procedure that most anyone will need to know to participate in the typical meeting following the rules.

It is good that the task of learning Parliamentary Procedure can be made easier because many have complained of its difficulty but this functional and practical approach results in a greater good. By it, the rules are made infinitely more useful. Robert wrote his rules about 100 years ago. They were based on the accepted practices of organized societies of that day and also on what had been written by earlier parliamentarians, particularly Thomas Jefferson, who wrote his "Manual of Parliamentary Practice" another century before that. Some updating is in order, updating of the sort that inevitably results when we consider a reasonable application of these rules in a meeting today. Good examples are the rules governing the amendment of motions. As Robert set them down, they appear stiff, formal and inflexible. Approached from the standpoint of their real purpose and their best uses in a contemporary American group, they need not be so. In an American group, sensitive to the needs of democratic group action and skilled in the practices of democracy, they can be interpreted in ways to provide a procedural method by which the true ends of democracy can uniquely be served. This is demonstrated in Lesson 6. For the present, we need only point out that (as illustrated in this lesson), we see how what is often dismissed as a rather unsatisfactory form of parliamentary debate can become parliamentary discussion in the contemporary sense, how alternate solutions to problems can be considered and the best selected, and how under the Rules a decision can be made more by a true consensus and less by the "yes" or "no" vote of a majority to a fixed proposition.

In a quite different way, the rules set down by Robert on the motion to postpone indefinitely, interpreted in the light of the needs of a contemporary organization, can provide a procedure of great utility. This motion, generally misunderstood and often forgotten and lost, as we point out in Lesson 5, provides a way by which an organization may drop a proposal without making a commitment to it—for or against. In these days of mass communications and publicity and a sensitivity of many organizations to their public image, this can be important.

The motion "to table" with its antiquated language, accurate in another day when there was a table and a clerk who could lay a motion there, is another problem. It is so, however, only until we have researched into its true purposes and begin thinking of these in terms of today's groups. As we point out in Lesson 9, there is a purpose which any contemporary society will regularly want served—a means to put aside a proposal in the form in which it can be taken up later, conveniently. Here we see that we need the motion "to table." Here we learn that if we do not permit this motion to be perverted deviously in its uses, as is the frequent and unfortunate present practice, it can be an invaluable parliamentary tool.

There are many other examples that could be cited from the pages that follow, but these three illustrate both the approach of this book, and the value of that approach. It is written on a premise which it demonstrates that we do not need to abandon the rules, as some suggest. We do not need to change the rules as some have tried. We need only to learn how to adapt them to our present needs and, happily, in so doing we gain the added dividend that the task of learning them is made easier.

Lesson 1:
Introduction

All of us should understand the basic facts of parliamentary procedure. All of us attend meetings. In this country all meetings are organized and conducted according to parliamentary rules.

Most people come into contact with simple parliamentary rules about the time they become Cub Scouts or Brownies. Even organizations of small children occasionally put questions to a vote. Many grade schools have club activities. Again, simple parliamentary routines are followed. High schools organize student councils, clubs of many kinds, and sometimes sororities and fraternities. Colleges and universities are rich in student organizations. In the world outside school, labor unions, political parties, professional organizations, and other special-interest groups of a hundred kinds carry on their business according to parliamentary procedure. So do boards of directors; so do legislative bodies; so do fraternal societies and clubs.

We have been described as a nation of joiners. Or, as Will Rogers put it, "when more than six people get a prejudice somebody organizes it and makes them pay dues." Americans may join for the sake of joining, but they also join for more worthwhile reasons. Doctors promote their professional interests and their concerns for public health in the American Medical Association. Lawyers become members of the American Bar Association. Professors join the American Association of University Professors. Each profession and each specialty of it has its organizations. For the nonprofessional there are unions—AFL, CIO, UAW, and many others. One of these organizations is likely to be a part of any life in America. There are still others most do not escape. One of these is the grade and high school PTA. And people alert and alive to their responsibilities in their communities and the democratic society in which they live will join political and civic clubs, church groups, and perhaps the NAACP, the SPCA, or the WCTU. So it is almost certain that you will someday belong to some organized groups. You will attend meetings in which you will want to take part. To do so you must have some knowledge of the procedure they follow. This is parliamentary procedure.

The term *parliamentary procedure* is usually understood by Americans as a method of conducting business in the manner prescribed in a small book called *Robert's Rules of Order*. Most American organizations are legally bound to follow these *Rules* because their constitutions require it, usually in an article specifying "*Robert's Rules of Order* shall govern the conduct of the meetings of this society."

How Robert's Rules of Order came to be synonymous with American parliamentary practice is an interesting story. Actually General Robert did not invent parliamentary procedure or the rules governing its practice. The first edition of *Robert's Rules* was published in 1874. Thousands of years before that date men began to realize that there must be a better way of getting people to work together than jungle law, in which the strong pushed the weak around and the weak cowered in fear. There is evidence that the notion that rules were needed to protect the rights of all first found expression among ancient tribes of Germany. First specific credit for an orderly system can be given to King Edgar, the first ruler of united England. We know that more than a thousand years ago, in 959, he instituted an elementary system that spelled out a way by which individuals with conflicting interests could gather under one roof, resolve their differences, and make decisions in a democratic way—without resorting to fists, clubs, or pitched battles. There was no secretary who handed down the minutes of these first organized meetings, and history does not tell us much about their immediate success. It is possible that in the beginning King Edgar had to bump a few heads together, perhaps crack a few skulls; but we know from the results that his subjects caught onto the idea that certain rules could protect by peaceful means the rights of every man—rights he held simply because he was a man.

Like all good ideas, this one spread, and the rules of order were strengthened and expanded. Within three centuries the English parliament had come into being; from it we get the term *parliamentary procedure.* Our forefathers brought parliamentary procedure with them, and our colonial legislatures followed it. Thomas Jefferson wrote *A Manual of Parliamentary Procedure* for the first Continental Congress. In the years that followed, others wrote similar manuals, most of them intended primarily to guide the proceedings of Congress and other legislative bodies.

In 1874 General Henry Robert, an army engineer who had made a lifetime study of group procedures, finished his first edition of what he called *Rules of Order.* This was intended to provide a code of rules, based generally on the procedure of our Congress, which could be adopted by voluntary societies. The original edition was revised and expanded many times up to 1915 when it was published under the title *Robert's Rules of Order Revised.* This is the book most organizations live by today.

The general acceptance of General Robert's *Rules* during the last eighty years shows that there was a real need for a common parliamentary practice. Imagine the confusion if each time we joined a new group we faced a new set of rules! Or imagine the problems, if every time we formed a new organization we had to make a set of rules!

We are greatly indebted to General Robert. This no one questions, but many find his book difficult and his Rules hopelessly complex. This is true particularly for the beginner because Robert's book is not a book from which the procedure can easily be learned. General Robert did not write a textbook. As he put it, he wrote "a very brief but exhaustive set of rules of order to be adopted by societies," adding that if it "were adapted to the needs of the student, it would not be suitable for adoption as the rules of order of the society." To try to learn parliamentary procedure from this exhaustive set of rules is like trying to learn football from the official NCAA rules or trying to learn to drive an automobile from the hundreds of traffic statutes.

Unlike *Robert's Rules,* this book *is* intended to be a textbook. It is not a restatement of the rules or even a textbook of the rules. It is a textbook on the procedure that results when the rules are followed. It is not a book for anyone whose prime concern is to know the rules—a parliamentarian. It is for one interested in becoming an effective member (or presiding officer) in groups, following the rules.

If you think this is a distinction without a difference, you should know that you can be a very effective member or even a competent presiding officer without knowing all the rules. Many of them are never used in most organizations. Many others are rarely used. Nine tenths of the business of most societies is taken care of with a few of them.

For this book we have simply selected those procedures by which the typical voluntary society will transact its business if it follows accepted practice. There are first the motions used in the handling of business—about a dozen of them. Then there are what we have called the special emergency procedures, by which members protect their rights and privileges—six of them. Each of these items has been made the subject of a lesson showing its use. We have added lessons on how to preside as chairman, how to form a new organization, how to write a constitution, some exercises for practicing what you have learned, and finally a list of the most useful books to go to if you would learn more.

Lesson 2:
The Core Procedure

How Parliamentary Procedure Provides Order. The purpose of parliamentary procedure is to provide a method by which groups may effectively and properly achieve their aims. Effectively means efficiently—that is, without confusion, wasted time, or wasted effort. Properly here means democratically, and this means in a way suited to the sensibilities of men in a society that respects human dignity and the rights and privileges of all.

Efficiency begins with order, which, the philosophers tell us, is nothing more than arrangement suited to the purpose; and this arrangement under parliamentary procedure begins with the physical arrangement of the meeting itself. We put a chairman up front in charge, or presiding as we say, and we group the members out in front in the classroom style with which you are already familiar. This has come down to us from the days when King Edgar, and before him some German tribal chief, sat up front on his throne and those assembled grouped themselves about him. And we know that the term *chairman* derives from the fact that in these early days the members stood or sat on the floor (or ground) and the chairman was so called because he was the only one who had a chair on which to sit. All now have chairs, but we have not improved upon this basically orderly arrangement, probably because it is one well-suited to the purpose. We may vary this physical arrangement somewhat by being seated around a long table with the chairman at the head, or sometimes even in a less formal circle; but always we keep the essential ordering feature of the chairman at a focal point for the membership.

Given this physical arrangement we place the chairman in charge. We delegate to him the authority and assign him the duty of enforcing the ground rules we have adopted and agreed to live by.

At the very heart of what we have agreed upon is a common formula for the treatment of every piece of business that comes before our group. We call it the *core procedure*. It is illustrated by the following typical dialogue.

> *Chairman:* Is there any business (or further business) to come before this meeting?
> *Member* (rising): Mr. Chairman.
> *Chairman:* Mr. Jones.
> *Member:* I move that we initiate a campaign to increase our membership.
> *Second member:* I second the motion.
> *Chairman:* It has been moved and seconded that we initiate a campaign to increase our membership. Is there any discussion?

This proposal or motion is now "the business before the house," for its single and undivided attention until disposed of. There will normally be a discussion of its merits until the chairman may say:

> *Chairman:* If there is no further discussion, we shall now vote. The motion is that we initiate a campaign to increase our membership. All those in favor, raise your right hand. All those opposed. The motion is carried (*or lost*).

We will call this typical dialogue the core procedure because it illustrates the six typical steps in the orderly presentation and disposition of a piece of business. It is at the heart and core of the process because each step helps to make good order possible.

1. A member rises and is "recognized" by the chairman. He has the floor and only he may speak.
2. The member proposes a motion. This provides a precise statement of the proposition before the house.

3. The motion is "seconded," so we know that at least one other member believes the motion deserves consideration.
4. The motion is restated by the chairman to indicate it is in order and open for discussion.
5. The motion is put to a vote to learn the will of the assembly.
6. The vote is announced to indicate the decision, and that the matter is settled.

Given the physical arrangement of the chairman at a focal point with the members in front or around him, and given this core procedure, we have the basis for the order which it is the purpose of parliamentary procedure to provide. But the procedure must be more than orderly—it must also be democratic, "suited to the sensibilities of men in a society that respects human dignity and the rights and privileges of all."

If we were willing to settle for order alone, we might make the chairman an autocrat and a dictator and let him make his own rules. Democracy, however, calls for the observance of some basic principles. For democratic decision-making and action in groups, there are four that are vital:

1. The rights of each member must be equal to the rights of all.
2. Freedom of speech must be assured, in full and free debate.
3. The rights of minorities must be protected.
4. The will of the majority must be carried out.

It is to make operative in a group these four basic principles that we use parliamentary procedure and abide by *Robert's Rules*. Where there is confusion and chaos there can be no democracy. The procedure provides order. Each of the rules, in some way, makes its own contribution of something essential to democratic action. All together they guarantee equal rights, free debate, minority protection, and majority rule.

Lesson 3:
The Main Motion

How to Present a Proposal.   The first and most important procedure in parliamentary practice is the main motion. It is the
means by which substantive business of an organization is transacted. It is used by a member to introduce a proposal that he
thinks deserving of the consideration of the assembly. Why this
form is used and how it is handled we have already illustrated
in the typical dialogue in Lesson 3, outlining the core procedure.

When you are a member of an organization you have a responsibility in all that it does, a duty to exert your proper influence in its affairs. The first step toward effective participation
in meetings is mastering the procedure for proposing the doing
of the things you think should be done. As you learned in
Lesson 2, your proposals must be presented in the form of
motions. To so phrase them usually calls for special skill, technique, and know-how. The first three words of a motion are fixed.
The accepted and proper form is "I move that . . ." The form "I
move you . . ." is sometimes heard, but it is archaic and provin-
cial. And to say "I make a motion that . . ." is awkward and does
violence to the language. What follows the three little words
deserves some thought because you must state here precisely
what you propose, in a single sentence without footnotes, hem-
ming and hawing, or parenthetical explanations. The motion must
be so stated that all will understand it, that someone will be
encouraged to second it, and the chairman will be able to repeat
it. It must also be worded so that after it is passed, it will bring
about the doing of what you want done—no more, no less.

The essential qualities for the statement of a main motion are
clarity, brevity, precision (accuracy), simplicity, and complete-
ness. The need for clarity as opposed to ambiguity is obvious
because what you propose must be understood and if possible
be immediately intelligible when it is proposed. Brevity is neces-
sitated by the limitations of the procedure. Both the assembly
and the chairman need something short enough to be conveniently handled in the discussion. Precision and accuracy are essen-

tial because what you propose will often become a formal enactment of a piece of legislation with effects on many for a long future. It may at the same time be a set of instructions that will be carried out as you intend only if the language of your motion is accurate. Finally, the motion should be stated as simply as possible. Simplicity saves time and prevents misunderstanding and confusion. The following examples of poorly phrased motions will help to clarify the points just stated:

I move that we change our meeting time to a later hour so we can start on time. (*Bad*)

I move that our meeting time be changed to 8:30 p.m. (*Good*)

I move that we take some action on the problems of juvenile delinquency in this town. (*Bad*)

I move we appoint a committee to study our local problem of juvenile delinquency and to make recommendations for a course of action for consideration at our next meeting. (*Good*)

I move we spruce up this shabby clubroom with some new furniture to replace the junk we now have, especially a desk and chair for the president. (*Bad*)

I move we buy a new desk and chairs for this club room. (*Good*)

I move that we donate to the Community Fund. (*Bad*)

I move that we donate $25 to the Community Fund (*Good*)

The last example illustrates one of the most common violations of the principles of good wording of motions. As we have said, a motion should be complete—it should say all that is necessary. If you have attended meetings, you know that chairmen are regularly faced with motions to make donations that do not specify how much, motions to hold picnics that do not set a date—motions that do not specify what, how, when, or where. These always create problems and usually confusion. A well-worded motion is clear, brief, precise, simple, and complete.

Another problem related to motions sometimes arises when an

eager but misguided member, apparently bent on doing business two things at a time, proposes a motion such as the following:

I move that we invite the mayor to speak at the next meeting, and send delegates to our national convention.

This is an obvious violation of the principle of parliamentary procedure that the attention of the assembly must be confined to one thing at a time. This principle requires that a motion be single in the sense of embodying a single, unified purpose and objective. Because what we have above is really two proposals, they call for two motions separately proposed and considered. Sometimes, however, what may at first sight be two is a single one poorly worded. Take the following, for example:

I move that we buy new furniture and raise the dues.

What this member had in mind was the following:

I move that we buy new furniture for our clubroom and pay for it by raising our dues.

So stated, this motion might pass the "one thing at a time" test, and it probably should because the proposer (bless him) does not skip the too-often-neglected problem of how the money should be raised.

Our consideration of the effective wording of motions would not be complete without giving some attention to those that go beyond the prescribed routine and immediate purposes and powers of a group. Organizations, particularly in America, often want to make themselves heard and their influence felt on community and national issues. They find particularly useful the wordings that give motions the special forms we call *petitions, recommendations,* and *resolutions.* This is also true for student and campus organizations whose interests and concerns will range widely and sometimes far beyond the specific purposes stated in their constitutions. It is also true for many other societies and associations in certain situations, as we shall see below.

When a student organization wants to engage a speaker for a meeting, propose a party, sponsor a program, or do anything else that comes directly within its purposes and powers, it makes sense simply "to move that" it do these things. On the other hand, when a student organization wants a university administration to abolish final examinations or provide more parking or to relax dormitory rules, it does not make sense "to move that" the university do these things because the students cannot "move" the university. Good wording of the motion in this case calls for the use of *petition*. Examples of such motions are the following:

I move that we petition the university to provide more student parking.

I move that we petition the Dean of Arts and Sciences to abolish final written examinations.

I move that we petition the Dean of Students to extend the dormitory curfew to 2 a.m. on weekends.

We can use the petition form effectively when we want something done that we may appropriately ask from some governing or administrative authority that is charged with the responsibility in the matter. Students may petition the dean, taxpayers may petition the legislature, and citizens' groups may petition town and county boards and the common councils of cities.

Sometimes instead of being in a position to petition, an organization may be more appropriately in a position to *recommend*. A student booster club might recommend to the athletic board that the price of the season tickets be dropped. A PTA might recommend to the school superintendent that the lunch period be extended or the school day shortened. Most particularly, the committee of an organization charged with investigating a problem or studying a proposal might recommend a course of action. Typical examples of recommendations are the following:

I move that we recommend that the price of a season ticket to all athletic contests be reduced to $10.

I move that we recommend to our national convention that our dues be lowered.

I move that this committee recommend to our organization that our lease on this clubhouse should not be renewed for next year.

Wingate College Library

There is still another category of action, in which we can neither take the action directly ourselves nor ask it of someone or recommend it, but can publicly express ourselves in favor of it. The parliamentary device used here is called a *resolution,* typically initiated as follows:

I move that we go on record in favor of lowering the voting age to 18.

I move that we go on record in favor of tuition-free college education for all Americans.

I move that we go on record in support of the reform candidate for mayor.

The key phrase in a resolution is "go on record," which is to say, "let it be a matter of record." This wording makes it possible for us to frame this type of proposal into a motion logically suited to an organization in which, otherwise, we would be hard put to state it sensibly.

If you read the daily newspapers you know that in this land of democracy and freedom of speech, organizations of all kinds regularly adopt resolutions. They do it to clarify and define their stand on issues and to let it be known, so their influence will be felt. National conventions of the American Legion, American Medical Association, Daughters of the American Revolution, and so on adopt resolutions on national defense, health, education— all sorts of things. Because it is usually intended that a resolution will be publicized beyond the meeting that adopts it, and perhaps sent to places of influence for action, it is usually embellished beyond the simple statement as furnished in our illustration above. In such cases the bare statement is prefaced by some persuasive argument (—that is, the reasoning behind the proposal) as illustrated in the following example.

Whereas the death toll on our highways shows an alarming increase, and

Whereas stricter law enforcement is the most effective way to reduce highway accidents, and

Whereas our Governor has submitted a proposal for more effective law enforcement in this state, therefore be it

Resolved that we go on record as favoring the Governor's highway speed control bill.

Typical resolutions will carry two or three statements of arguments or reasoning prefixed by *Whereas* as illustrated above, and sometimes they will carry an additional praragraph or two specifying the action to be taken. To the one above, for example, there might be added "and be it further resolved that a copy of this resolution be forwarded to the governor, the state legislature, and the newspapers." In certain ordinary matters of business it may be advantageous for a motion to be more formally worded for the record and to carry with it the reasons for its adoption. Here the resolution has legitimate and important uses. A formal resolution is usually better suited than a simple main motion to express the niceties and courtesies. Resolutions, therefore, are regularly used to read into the record appreciation for services rendered and condolences for members departed. Resolutions are also an ideal and regularly used medium for expressing censure and commendation.

A member wishing to propose a formal resolution will usually have it typed out in duplicate ahead of time, and when there is an opportunity to present it he prefaces the reading with the following:

I move the adoption of the following resolution. . . .

He proceeds then to read the resolution. If it is seconded, he hands one copy to the chairman or secretary for reference during its consideration and for the record if it is passed. Beyond this, the procedure for a resolution is the same as for any other main motion, using the core procedure.

After you have proposed a motion, it has been seconded, and it has been restated by the chairman for discussion, your proposal is entitled to full consideration. The entire attention of the assembly is upon it, and the spotlight is on you because this is your motion. You have a prior right to the floor, and this is

where you are expected to have your first say. You have proposed something that you feel deserves consideration. You have
your reasons. They should now be heard.

To be heard effectively in a meeting, either in your initial
speech on a motion you make or in any other speaking involves,
first of all, some knowledge of the limitations the *Rules* impose
on this kind of speaking. All of your remarks must be addressed
to the chair. They must be in the third person. They must be
germane to the immediately pending motion. Normally you must
deliver them standing in your place. They must be courteous,
and references to personalities are out of order. Parliamentary
speaking involves further an appreciation of several common-
sense observations. Most important among these is that speeches
should always be brief. The speaker in a meeting has not been
invited to make a speech. He has asked for and been given the
floor. He holds it on the assumption that what he is saying is
significant and of more consequence than what might otherwise
be said in the same time by another member.

Common sense argues also that effective speaking in most
meetings will be informative and persuasive rather than contentious and argumentative. In most voluntary societies and
groups the members do not divide themselves sharply and perma-
nently on the bases of parties. Seldom do they split, taking fixed
sides to debate a question. Rather they discuss a problem, speaking, listening, raising objections, and asking questions—even
amending the original proposal—in a common effort by reasonable men to reach a meeting of the minds.

Lesson 4:
The Structure of Parliamentary Procedure

How to Picture the Total Process.   To be unable to see the
forest because of the trees is every man's problem in learning
parliamentary procedure. This inevitably happens when he takes
up *Robert's Rules Revised* and begins with its table of forty-four
motions and its seven columns of rules, "answering 300 questions
in parliamentary practice." At the outset he is lost amid the

bewildering confusion of details, most of which have no perti-
nence to what most groups actually do.

In practice the procedure of most meetings goes little beyond
what you have already learned in the preceding pages. Most
business is transacted within the core procedure as we have
outlined it. Motions are proposed, discussed, and voted upon.
This basically is what meetings are for, and this is the ordinary
routine. It is only when we depart from the usual routine that
the other procedures come into use. Occasionally we may wish
to modify a motion, in which case we propose an amendment.
Sometimes we wish to give a proposal special study, in which
case we propose the motion to refer to a committee. Occasionally
we wish to postpone or set aside motions temporarily, or to drop
them, in which case we make use of the motions to postpone and
table.

In these instances, instead of the usual motion–discussion–
decision process in handling a proposal, we propose to "sidetrack"
it by one of these subsidiary motions, as they are called. They
are listed in *Robert's Rules* and most parliamentary charts like
this:

1. The motion to lay on the table.
2. The motion to postpone definitely.
3. The motion to refer to a committee.
4. The motion to amend.
5. The motion to postpone indefinitely.

In rare instances, instead of proceeding in the usual fashion
through the full, free, and unlimited discussion that usually takes
place before a motion is voted, an assembly may find it desirable
or necessary to limit or end the discussion. For this, there are two
motions:

1. The motion to limit debate.
2. The motion to close debate (also called *previous question*).

If, after a question has been decided, the members change
their minds (or circumstances change their minds for them), the
assembly may reverse itself by

1. The motion to reconsider.
2. The motion to repeal (or rescind).

Finally, an assembly needs a way to recess, perhaps to rest or eat lunch, or to end the session, to come back another day. For these purposes, there are

1. The motion to recess.
2. The motion to adjourn.

You can develop a very useful mental picture of the parliamentary process from the following diagram, which puts each motion in the place where it is normally used.

Proposal ⟶ Consideration—Discussion—Debate ⟶ Decision ◀— Reversal

(1) Main Motion	(8) Lay on the Table	(2) Limit		(9) Reconsider
	(7) Postpone Definitely		Vote	
	(6) Refer to a Committee	or		
	(5) Amend	(3) Close		(10) Repeal
	(4) Postpone Indefinitely			

1. A piece of business is presented as a (1) main motion and usually simply discussed and voted.
2. The discussion may be (2) limited or (3) closed.
3. As it is being discussed a motion may be (4) postponed indefinitely, (5) amended, (6) referred to a committee, (7) postponed definitely, or (8) tabled.
4. After the decision the vote may be (9) reconsidered or (10) repealed.

The diagram shows the ten motions by which business is handled when the *Rules* are followed. On these the structure of the procedure is built. How and when to use each of them is the problem of the following lessons.

Lesson 5:
Postpone Indefinitely

A proposal placed before an assembly is usually discussed and voted upon. It may also be disposed of in other ways by any one of the five subsidiary motions listed in the diagram in the preceding lesson.

The first subsidiary motion is "to postpone indefinitely." If it is passed, the proposal is dropped. There are times when associations, societies, and clubs are faced with proposals they do not wish either to pass or to reject. It may be because a negative vote would be blunt affront to the proposer and that segment of the membership that is with him. It may be that such a rejection reported in the press to the public outside would have unfortunate implications. It may also be true that the most democratic disposition of a proposal may be that of taking no action, for or against it—that the consensus of the assembly is that it should not commit itself on the question. It is for these and similar situations that the motion to postpone indefinitely has come to be a part of parliamentary practice. The following dialogue shows how you can use it where there is a motion before the house that should be dropped.

Member (after recognition): I move that this motion be postponed indefinitely.

Chairman (after second): It has been moved and seconded that this motion be indefinitely postponed. Is there any discussion?

Chairman (after discussion): If there is no further discussion, the question is on indefinite postponement. All those in favor raise your hands. Those opposed. The vote is affirmative. The original motion is dropped. Is there any further business to come before the house?

The motion to postpone indefinitely may be used by the opponents of a proposal to get a test vote without risking passage. If indefinite postponement is carried the proposal will be dropped and their purpose achieved. If it is not carried they have a poll to use in assessing the need for further action. This devious use of this, or any other procedure, is not good because whenever the true purposes of any motion are perverted it loses its meaning. Its purpose and meaning are confused and the assembly will not know, in voting, what it is really voting to do.

Lesson 6:
  ### Amend

Of the five subsidiary motions, the motion to amend merits the most careful study by anyone who would participate effectively in meetings because to be used it must be thoroughly understood. When used effectively it makes possible the best democratic group activity. Why this is true is illustrated in the example following, in which the assembly has before it the main motion that "the monthly dues be raised to $10 a month."

Member (after recognition): I move to amend the motion by striking out $10 and substituting $8.

Chairman (after hearing second): It has been moved and seconded that we amend the motion by striking out $10 and substituting $8. Is there any discussion on the amendment?

By this motion the attention of the assembly is now shifted from the basic question, (in this case, that of raising the dues) to the amendment, (whether $8 is better than $10). The specific question now receives full consideration following the core procedure, through discussion and the vote. If the majority votes to substitute $8 for the $10, the proposal is revised and the motion before the house now becomes "that our dues be raised to $8 a month."

The possibility of amendment makes a better decision possible for many reasons. If, at this meeting, most of the members were agreed that there should be a raise in dues, but no more than a minority would go along with $10, we see how the amendment process can solve the problem. Through the amendment process we can seek a better solution, one that can be tailored, if not to the unanimous taste of the group or a complete consensus, at least to the point of substantial majority support. This is good because it makes for happier and more contented members and therefore more effective organizational functioning. It is good also because it makes possible decisions and action that are more democratic in that they are acceptable to a greater number.

The business of a group operating democratically should be everybody's business. This means that each member should assess the group's problems, that each should be able to propose his solutions and to modify those selected, and, ideally at least, that all should come to agreement in selecting what is to be done. This is quite different from the opposite approach, in which the king, premier, emperor, superintendent, general manager, president, dean, quarterback, or boss issues an edict, promulgates a law, sends out a set of orders or a memorandum, calls the signals, or simply announces what is going to be done. For some operations this way has its advantages. For others the democratic way has values, and in the management of certain areas of human affairs these values are of first importance.

As we have said above, the business of a group operating democratically is everybody's business. This creates the unique problem in the old saying that "everybody's business is nobody's business." This is a problem for which good parliamentary practice can be the solution. In a well-run group, which means one using *Robert's Rules* intelligently, all of the business can be an effective concern of each member. If you and every other member will really work at it, the results are likely to be something that will give lie to the claims for authoritarianism, and autocracy. This is true if the procedure is intelligently used, and this applies most particularly, to the use of the amendment procedure.

It is the purpose of the discussion to give the assembly an opportunity to learn what should be done about the proposal. As a minimum, each member should exert his appropriate influence in the form of support for, or opposition to the proposal, by contributing pertinent information and by raising searching questions. But if the decision is to be a truly democratic one, each member should be able to affect more than the "yes" or "no" outcome. This he can do with amendments.

When a motion is presented it is often one man's idea of a course of action that should be taken to solve a problem the group faces. If two heads are better than one, then, to a certain extent, more heads are better than less, and the more brains we can bring to bear on the solution the better. In the amendment process each member of an assembly is provided a way in which he can bring his judgment and good sense to bear on the details and therefore the nature of the solution.

In the parliamentary situation considered earlier, in which a member had proposed that "to strengthen our treasury we raise our dues to $10 a month" it may be that you believe the assembly should consider the alternate solution of an assessment against the members to strengthen the treasury. You might proceed as follows:

Member (after recognition): I move to amend the motion by striking out the words "raise our dues to $10" and substituting "assess each member $20."

Chairman (after a second): It has been moved and seconded to amend the motion by striking out the words "raise our dues to $10" and substituting "assess each member $20." Discussion is now in order on the amendment.

This is an alternate solution for the problem of the main motion, which is how to get more money. There is no limit to the number of such solutions that might be suggested as long as they are germane—that is, in point and related to the proposal. What this rule means and how it is to be applied in such case is a problem for the chairman and will be considered later in this book. You need only remember that if you have an alternate proposal that you believe to be a better solution, you may—and we might add that you should—propose it as an amendment.

In addition to selecting the best solution or improving a good one by compromise, we can, through the procedure of amending, achieve the simpler and more obvious purposes of clarifying, correcting, revising, and perfecting proposals. In the situation we have been using for illustration, it may be that the motion to raise the dues needs clarification as to when the raise is to become effective. This would be true in the case of an organization in which it is customary for the members to pay their dues only quarterly or annually. In this case it might be necessary to correct, or at least clarify, by a motion to amend by adding the words "effective January 1st," so that the motion would read "that we raise our dues to $10 a month, effective January 1st."

In addition to these ordinary and what we might call basically proper and legitimate purposes of amendment, there are others quite different that are permitted by the rules. They are quite different in that it may be the intention of the proposer of the amendment to change the motion so that it will be rejected or so that the intent of the original motion will be reversed. These are called "hostile" amendments. If you will use your imagination to fill in the background that gave rise to the situation that precipitated the following excerpt from the transcribed minutes of what might be any politically alert and active organization in any community, both the purposes and the method of this sort of an amendment will be clear.

Chairman: The resolution before the house is that we commend the activities of our vice-president in support of the incumbent candidate for mayor. Is there any discussion?

Member (after recognition): I move to amend the resolution by striking out the word "commend" and substituting the word "condemn."

Chairman (after second): It has been moved and seconded to amend the resolution by striking out the word "commend" and substituting the word "condemn." Discussion is now in order on the amendment.

At first thought you may feel that this amendment ought to be ruled out of order on the ground that it is not germane, since it is completely at variance with the original motion. Actually it is not, if you take the more correct view that it is the broad purpose of the motion that must be considered. Here the broad purpose of the proposer of the original resolution was to get from the assembly an expression of its attitude and reaction to the political activities of the vice-president. He has asked for a pat on the back. The real answer, arrived at democratically, may be at the opposite end of the scale—a kick in the pants.

In the same way that we can amend the original motion, we

can also amend an amendment. That this may, at times, be useful will be obvious from the study of the following dialogue.

Member (after recognition): I move that we send two delegates to our national convention.

Chairman (after second): It has been moved and seconded that we send two delegates to our national convention. Is there any discussion?

Second member (after recognition): I move to amend the motion by adding the words "with all expenses paid."

Chairman (after second): It has been moved and seconded to amend the motion by adding the words "with all expenses paid." Discussion is now in order on the amendment.

Third member (after recognition): I move to amend the amendment by adding "except food, drink, and entertainment."

Chairman (after second): It has been moved and seconded to amend the amendment by adding the words "except food, drink and entertainment" after "expenses." Discussion is now in order on the amendment to the amendment.

A "primary" amendment provides an orderly way in which a proposal may be modified in the interests of wiser and more democratic decisions and action. In a similar way the "secondary" amendment, amending the primary amendment, may also serve good purposes. In this instance, when we are considering whether or not to pay the delegates' expense, it may be reasonable to consider whether these should include food, drink, and entertainment.

We have already called this amendment to the amendment a secondary amendment and the amendment to the original motion a primary one. We can add that tertiary amendments are not permitted. You can amend an amendment, but not an amendment is in order. But to participate effectively every member on the ground that a secondary amendment goes far enough—to go farther would involve the assembly in hopeless complexity.

It is the problem of the chairman to decide whether an amendment is in order. But to participate effectively every member should know the basic principles. These may be quickly stated. The first is that when an original motion is pending an amend-

ment must propose to change or modify it, and when an amendment is pending the secondary amendment must propose a
modification of the amendment (not of the original motion). If,
for example, there is a proposal before the house to repaint your
meeting room and someone moves to modify that by adding the
word "green," you could not at this particular point move to
include a refinishing of the floor. The immediately pending question is on the selection of the color for the repainting. The refinishing of the floor has to do with the original proposal of
redecorating the room and must therefore be proposed when the
original motion is immediately pending. A proper secondary
amendment at the point where "green" is being considered would
propose the insertion of the word "light" before the word "green."

Accepting Amendments. The amendment process can be
made more useful through a shortcut, by-passing the formalities
of the conventional amendment process. In certain situations
this will save time and also simplify the process. First let us see
an illustration of the procedure; then we can consider its special
utility. Let us return to our original example of the conventional
amendment procedure involving the motion to raise the dues
to $10.

Chairman: It has been moved and seconded that we raise our dues
to $10 a month. Is there any further discussion?

Member (after recognition): I move to amend the motion by adding
the words "effective January 1st."

Second member (the proposer of the motion): I accept the amendment.

Chairman: The proposer accepts the amendment. If there is no objection, the amendment is approved and the motion now before the
house is that we raise our dues to $10 a month effective January 1st.
Any further discussion?

Amendments suggesting obvious corrections are not the only
ones that proposers may sometimes wisely accept. In our original
illustration in this lesson the proposer of the motion to raise the
dues to $10 might wisely decide, after he has sensed the temper
of the assembly from the discussion, to accept the amendment
substituting $8 in the interests of achieving his purpose of getting

the dues raised. This variation in the conventional amendment procedure has, therefore, at least these two things to recommend it. It has strategic uses and it is time saving.

Filling Blanks. A sharp variation from that used in conventional amendment procedure for modifying a motion is the procedure called *amendment by creating and filling blanks.* Consider the situation of the Ladies' Coffee and Conversation Club discussing a motion to redecorate the clubroom in beige and green. There may well be as many suggestions for color combinations as there are ladies present. The essential question of whether or not to redecorate can get lost in the details of the choice of colors. The conventional amendment procedure will not serve well in the selection of the best color from many suggestions because the voting proceeds by a choice from two at a time. Amending by creating blanks comes to the rescue in this situation as follows:

Member (after recognition): I move to amend the motion, creating a blank by striking out the words "beige and green."

Chairman (after second): It has been moved and seconded that we amend by striking out the words "beige and green" to create a blank in the original motion. All those in favor of the motion, raise your hands. Those opposed. Motion is carried. Suggestions are now in order for filling the blank.

The chairman then proceeds by hearing and listing all of the suggestions and then taking a show of hands on each color until one receives a majority. When this has been done, the assembly proceeds in the usual way to consider the vote on the amended motion.

Amending to create a blank may be useful in any situation where there are many possible alternatives, such as sums of money, dates, or names. In a motion calling for the donation of a certain sum to the local United Fund there may be many opinions as to the amount of the sum. The motion to hold the annual club picnic on May fifth may bring forth preferences for many other dates. The motion to send John Smith as the delegate to the annual convention in Miami may prompt the suggestion of several others who might be sent. In each of these cases the decision may be more easily and at the same time more democratically arrived at if the procedure of filling the blanks is used.

In all of our illustrations of amendments and our discussion of them thus far we have considered only amendments to original main motions. This is not to imply that amendments may not be applied to other kinds of motions, particularly some of the subsidiary motions listed in Lesson 4. It may be useful, for example, to amend the motion to refer to a committee by changing the number of members on it, or to amend the motion to postpone a proposal until three o'clock by changing the time, or to amend the motion to limit debate by changing the limit. This may be done, and in the conventional way. The general rule is that on any motion in which there are choices available an amendment may be proposed.

Rules for Amendments. Many rather confusing rules have been written to determine whether a particular amendment is in order and may be considered at a certain time. Parliamentarians, following Robert and his rules, have tried to supply the answers by saying there are three ways to amend: (1) by addition, (2) by subtraction and (3) by substitution. This is not very helpful since all it says is that you can add something, take something out, or do both. As a member you should assume that it is the responsibility of the chairman to decide when an amendment is or is not in order. The only limitations that he can properly apply to amendments are practical and common-sense ones. You can change a proposal any way you want as long as you do not depart from its purpose. *You can change a proposal, but you cannot propose to interchange it with another.* The principle that should guide you as a member is that if there is a proposal before the house for which you would suggest a modification in the interests of the purposes of the group, you have both the right and duty to suggest it. If you are in error, the chairman will tell you so.

Instead of thinking in terms of addition, subtraction, and substitution as the methods of amending, it is much more useful to think in terms of amending by editing. The best way, and in fact the only way, an amendment can be handled in an assembly is through an approach to the original motion like that of a copy reader to copy he is correcting. He edits the sentences of the copy so that the typesetter will know precisely what is wanted. He crosses out and adds specific words with his pencil. You should do the same mentally and orally, using the specific words as we have illustrated in our examples. In so doing you give the chairman specific instructions, and what you want done will be clear to your fellow members.

Lesson 7:
Refer to a Committee

Our concern in this lesson is how a proposal may be referred to a committee—that is, turned over to a small, special study group of several members to achieve a needed, or careful, or thorough, or more private and special investigation before action is finally taken on it. The procedure is as follows.

Member (after recognition): I move to refer the motion before the house to a study committee to report at our next meeting.

Chairman (after second): It has been moved and seconded to refer the motion to a committee. Any discussion? . . . All in favor of referring the question to a committee, raise your hands. Those opposed. The motion is carried. The question is referred to a committee. Is there any further business?

The best illustration of the usefulness of the committee procedure is found in the Congress of the United States. There it is often said that everything is done in committee. Congress has the biggest job in the world, that of running the country. The Senate and House find that the only way to get the job done is to refer proposals to committees to study them and to make recommendations to the general assemblies.

The need for the committee procedure in any organization will vary directly with its size and the amount of business to be handled. Its usefulness on a particular piece of business in a smaller organization will depend on how willing and able the members are to make a decision on the matter immediately without more investigation and special study. In regular procedure a proposal is presented and the decision is made on the basis of the consideration that is provided in the discussion and debate that follows. This can provide only what the members already know and are willing to contribute from the floor. If it becomes apparent that this is not enough, that it leaves many questions unanswered and many of those present not prepared to decide, a study or research committee can be useful.

The committee procedure temporarily delays the decision on a motion by the assembly to permit research in books, consultation with experts and authorities, or any other measures that may prove helpful. When the work of a committee is completed and the results of its work are made available to the assembly in its report, the discussion can continue and a better-informed vote can be taken. Through the committee procedure the most interested and best minds may be brought to bear on a certain problem in the calm privacy of a smaller meeting, with a saving of time and effort for the whole assembly. A student group considering a proposal to invite a controversial speaker to the campus might refer this motion to a committee of several members charged with the specific responsibility of gathering from responsible officials of the university administration their reaction to the proposal. A large national association considering an invitation from a certain city as a place for its next national convention might refer the problem to a committee charged with making a "site visit" to look at the hotel, its meeting rooms, and other facilities.

Many organizations have regular permanent committees always in being, each charged with the responsibility for a certain class or type of business. These are called *standing committees*. Typical ones are committees on entertainment, finance, membership, constitution and by-laws. Where these exist, a proposal that may be properly considered the province of a given committee is usually referred to it, either at the direction of the chairman, or by a motion to that effect.

A further extension of this practice, widely used in America, particularly in large, professional associations, is called the *refer-*

ence committee procedure. All proposals coming from the club membership to the national convention, national council of delegates, or whatever the national legislative session is called, are submitted in advance for consideration to reference committees for study. These committees then make recommendations to the general meeting. Such organizations have learned through experience that this is the only way in which the tremendous volume of business of a large association can be effectively handled at a large national convention.

When you make the motion to refer a matter to a committee you should normally include specifications for the number of members it is to have, how they are to be selected, what exactly it is to do (if there are special instructions), and finally when it is to report. Committees are usually made up of an odd number of members—three, five, or perhaps even seven—to avoid tie votes. They are usually appointed by the chair, but they may be selected by nominations from the floor or by ballot. They usually report their progress or findings under the heading of old business at the next meeting.

On controversial questions the membership of a committee may take on special significance. A "loaded" committee can bring back "loaded" evidence and make biased recommendations. With this in mind, the opponent of a proposal might, in his motion to refer it to a committee, name its members, three or five persons, suited to his purposes. This is why it must be possible, as we pointed out earlier, to use the amendment process to modify a motion such as this. In this instance another member might move to amend the motion to refer to a committee so that it would provide for selecting the committee members by some other, more equitable means, such as election by the assembly or appointment by the chairman.

The committee process of delegating a proposal or proposition to a small group for particular study or action is used in another way in parliamentary procedure, as illustrated by the following:

Chairman: Is there any further new business to come before the meeting?

Member (after recognition): I move that a committee of five be appointed by the chairman to investigate the possibilities of finding a more suitable meeting place for this organization and report back at our next meeting.

Chairman (after second): It has been moved and seconded that we appoint a committee to investigate the possibilities of our finding a better meeting place for this organization and to report back at the next meeting. Is there any discussion?

You will note that this is not a subsidiary motion proposing some special treatment for a proposal or main motion but a proposal in itself—an original, main motion. Used in this way the motion to refer is in every sense a main motion and is subject to treatment as such. This may include full and free debate as well as being (1) dropped, (2) amended, (3) postponed, or (4) tabled.

Robert's Rules specify that committees themselves should follow good parliamentary practice, insofar as is possible; but common sense dictates that three or five persons will dispense with most of the formalities. A committee must have a chairman, and he should run things as the rules provide insofar as he finds this practical. It is his responsibility to see the task completed, and this will result only if he calls meetings and conducts them. And finally, he prepares the report on the results. The majority of a committee constitutes a quorum—that is, the number necessary to transact business at a meeting; and decisions of a committee are by majority vote. If a committee is empowered to take action (for example, find a speaker, hire a hall, or engage a dance band) it acts by majority vote. A study committee rendering a report will render a "majority report," but any of those dissenting may disagree and present a "minority report."

Committee Reports. Committee reports may be oral or written, formal or informal. They may be entirely informative, factual, objective, and without recommendations. On the other hand, they may be argumentative or persuasive, concluding with specific recommendations.

The problem of how to handle committee reports is one for the chairman and will be considered later. All that the committee member, particularly the chairman, needs to know is that he may expect to be called upon to report in the meeting specified, usually under the heading of unfinished business. Perhaps he

should also know that if the assembly is not satisfied with the
report of his committee the motion may be "recommitted" to his
group or, if the assembly wishes to go so far, it may discharge the
committee and appoint a new one with the hope of better results.

Lesson 8:
Postpone Definitely

When a proposal or main motion is being considered in a meeting, those present may wish to (1) drop it or to (2) amend it.
Or, as we have just seen, they may wish to (3) refer it to a
committee. The fourth possibility is that they may wish to postpone it to a specified later time. The procedure is illustrated in
the following.

Chairman: Is there any further discussion on the motion before the
house?

Member (after recognition): I move to postpone the motion before
the house until two o'clock.

Chairman (after second): It has been moved and seconded to postpone the motion before the house until two o'clock. Any discussion? . . .
All those in favor of postponement, raise your hands. All opposed. The
vote is in favor. The motion is postponed until two o'clock. Is there
any further business?

A main motion or proposal may be postponed until later in the
same meeting—until after lunch, until three o'clock, or until after
dinner. It may also be postponed until the next meeting, at which
it would come up under unfinished business. It is not normally in
order to postpone beyond the next regular session because this
might be equivalent to indefinite postponement and dropping the
proposal, unless there is a clearly proper and logical relationship
between the time suggested for the postponement and the motion
itself. For example, the organization might want to postpone a
proposal to donate toys for Christmas until the Christmas season,
or a proposal to levy an assessment against the members until
April, after income taxes are paid.

The usually good reasons for postponing a piece of business are
(1) that the time the proposal is being considered is not a good

one for some particular reason, or (2) the time suggested in the postponement is a better one for some reason. The present time may not be good because there are more urgent and pressing matters that ought to be disposed of. The future time may be a better one because the intervening time can provide an opportunity for thinking over the problem or getting the answers to some questions, or because there is likely to be a larger or more representative or more interested membership present at that time. There may be strategic reasons. The opponents of a proposal may seek to have it postponed because they feel they will have a better chance to beat it at a later time. The proponents of the proposal may seek to postpone with better hope of passage in mind.

As is normally the case under *Robert's Rules* the assembly decides by a majority vote not only whether a piece of business should be postponed, but also the details of the postponement. And this it may do by using the amendment procedure to change the day or hour specified in the motion.

A piece of business postponed to a certain time becomes what we call a *general order* for that time. It cannot be considered before that time unless the assembly reverses itself or suspends the rules by a two-thirds vote; and when the time comes, the assembly cannot refuse to consider it except by a two-thirds vote. If the motion has been postponed until three o'clock, for example, either at that hour or as soon thereafter as the pending business has been disposed of, the question is brought before the assembly by the chairman, who should be reminded of it by the secretary; and if all this fails, a member may simply "call for the orders of the day."

A piece of business postponed to a certain day and hour is an *order of the day* for that time, and it is usually called a *general order* to distinguish it from a variation of the procedure called a *special order*. A special order is used when the assembly wants to make absolutely sure that when the time comes the motion will be considered. A member may say:

I move that the motion before the house be postponed until this afternoon at three o'clock and be made a special order of the day for that time.

And if this motion is passed by the special vote of two-thirds, the matter becomes a special order for three o'clock. This means that at three o'clock the assembly drops whatever it is doing to take up the special order. This procedure has particular utility for large meetings and conventions, meeting over a period of several days, in which members are moving in and out of the hall. In such cases they want assurance that the right people will be present at a particular time, or that an important piece of business will be taken up at a certain time.

Creating Orders As Main Motions. The procedure of creating orders of the day by the motion for definite postponement has evolved a related procedure. This is illustrated by the following.

Chairman: Is there any further business?

Member (after recognition): I move that the question of amending our constitution to admit female members to this organization be made a special order of business for tomorrow morning at ten o'clock.

Chairman (after second): It has been moved and seconded that the question of amending our constitution to admit female members be made a special order of business for tomorrow morning at ten o'clock. Is there any discussion? . . . This takes a two-thirds vote. All those in favor, raise your hands. Those opposed. The motion is carried. The secretary will make a note of the fact that this motion is a special order of business for tomorrow morning at ten o'clock. Is there any further business?

The difference here is that this motion is an original proposal —a main motion, bringing up a new matter of business, and not a subsidiary motion arising out of another motion. This makes it subject to the rules applying to a main motion. It may be (1) dropped, (2) amended, (3) referred to a committee, (4) tabled, and it might even, with some logic, be (5) postponed definitely if it is possible that an assembly might wish for some strange reason to consider a bit later whether or not this special order should be created.

This same variation of creating orders of the day can be used to create general orders, and the use of both can be of particular value to a very busy national meeting gathering members from distant places. With general and special orders they can establish a rather definite agenda for disposing of a series of matters that must be attended to. By setting up a series of special orders to take care of the most urgent matters, judiciously placed through the duration of a convention, they will have some assurance that the work will be done, and some certainty that the time will not be frittered away on inconsequential things.

Lesson 9:
Lay on the Table

In the last lesson we learned how to postpone a motion to a better time by means of the motion to postpone definitely. In this lesson we shall learn how to postone a motion, not because we have a better time in mind, but simply because there is more urgent business to be considered at the present time. The procedure is the following.

Member (after recognition): I move the motion be laid on the table.

Chairman (after second): It has been moved and seconded that the question before the house be laid on the table. There is no discussion. All those in favor of tabling, raise your hands. Those opposed. The motion is carried. The question is tabled. Is there any further new business?

Some history of the unusual language of this motion will be helpful for your understanding of its uses and purposes. In British parliament and in our Congress and the early legislatures, the clerk of the house sat in the front of the room at a table upon which were stacked the bills (proposals) to come before the meeting. When a proposal was made the bill was "taken up from the table"—the bill was before the house for consideration, or as we would say, the motion was pending. After some debate the house might wish to return it to the table. As Thomas Jefferson put it in his *Manual of Parliamentary Procedure* (Section 33):

When the house has something else which claims its present attention but would be willing to reserve in their power to take up the proposition whenever it shall suit them, they order it to lie on their table; it may then be called for at any time.

It is the purpose of the motion to table, therefore, to enable an assembly to set aside temporarily the consideration of a proposal because something more urgent should be taken up, or possibly because this is not a particularly good time to carry on with it. You might move to table a motion dealing with your club's spring picnic because it is urgent that the meeting get to the business of selecting a speaker for the next meeting. You might move to table the motion proposing a very controversial change in your organization's membership requirement, so that you could move to take it from the table later in the day, or next meeting, when more members are likely to be present.

You can readily think of other similar uses for this procedure, but if they include using the motion as a quick and polite technique for having a motion dropped, you should banish the thought. To table is so often misused in American societies to kill a motion that many have come to believe that this is its proper purpose.

By this motion, as Jefferson put it, "they order it to lie on their table . . . willing to reserve in their power to take it up . . . whenever it shall suit them." When a motion is put on the table it is not put into the wastebasket. Two evils result if we use this motion as a convenient device for killing proposals. The first is that we lose it as a tool for achieving the purposes for which it is intended. In organizations where the motion to table becomes in fact a motion to kill, we have in fact lost the motion to table. The more serious evil is that when the motion to table is so perverted and misused, democratic processes are thwarted. Consider the situation in which very shortly after a proposal has been presented and seconded, and before its proponents have had an opportunity to exercise their rights to make a case for it, someone moves to lay it on the table. If this is passed, the right of the minority to full and free debate has been denied if the intent of the assembly, in so voting, is to drop the motion. This is true because the motion to table is undebatable. The proper procedure to drop a motion is the motion to postpone indefinitely. The motion to postpone indefinitely permits full and free debate, including under it any discussion that may involve the merits of the main motion.

The true purposes of the motion to lay on the table are served when it is proposed with the honest intent of taking up the matter at a later time. It is taken up at any time when the meeting is open for business, as follows:

Chairman: Is there any other business?

Member (after recognition): I move to take from the table the motion dealing with requirements for membership.

Chairman (after second): It has been moved and seconded to take from the table the motion dealing with the requirements for membership. All those in favor, raise your hands. Those opposed. It is carried. Will the secretary please read the motion?

It is obvious from this that there is no guarantee that a tabled motion will ever be taken up again, because someone must move to take it from the table and a majority must go along. Then too, a motion tabled is considered to remain on the table only until the end of the next meeting. If it is not taken up before the end of that time, it is in effect dropped. It can, of course, be brought up at a later time, but only as a matter of new business. There is some assurance that it will be taken up, however, in the rule that a motion to take from the table has a prior right over another main motion. This is to say that when the presiding officer asks for further business and another member rises and proposes a motion, you may rise immediately after and propose instead that a motion be taken from the table. If you do so, your motion will take precedence over the other and the chairman must put your motion to take from the table to a vote.

Summary: Lessons 5–9. In the preceding five lessons we have considered the following motions:

1. Lay on the table.
2. Postpone definitely.
3. Refer to a committee.
4. Amend.
5. Postpone indefinitely (drop).

These complete our list of subsidiary motions—so called because they may be applied to a motion as a subsidiary treatment. With their use a proposal (1) may be temporarily set aside to permit more urgent business to be taken up, (2) may be post-poned to a better or a set time, (3) may be given the special study that a committee can provide, (4) may be corrected, re-vised, or compromised by amendment, or (5) may be dropped—that is, indefinitely postponed without a vote for or against. Considered individually each of these subsidiary motions, prop-erly used, serves a particular need for any group, and each provides an orderly and a democratic way to meet that need. Collectively they provide adequate means to do anything an assembly might wish to do under almost any conceivable circum-stance and at any juncture in its affairs. And beyond this, as a kind of fringe benefit, they "sophisticate" group procedure in ways that make it more suited to people sensitive to the cour-tesies, the niceties, and the neatness and precision of good group action among ladies and gentlemen.

Lesson 10:
Limit Debate

Because organizations are made up of people, there will be times in meetings when procedures are needed to prevent mem-bers from abusing their rights to freedom of speech and the privilege of full and free debate guaranteed by *Robert's Rules.* There are two motions available: one to limit debate, the other to close it. In this lesson, we consider the first:

Chairman: Is there any further discussion?
Member (after recognition): I move that debate on this motion be limited to ten more minutes.
Chairman (after second): It has been moved and seconded that debate on the question before the house be limited to ten more min-utes. This motion is undebatable. All those in favor of so limiting debate, raise your hands. Those opposed. There being two-thirds in favor, debate will be closed in ten minutes and a vote will be taken at that time. The discussion may continue.

In its ancient beginnings common parliamentary practice al-lowed all motions to be fully debatable. There were no limitations because the right of debate is inherent in the very notion of a deliberative assembly. When you place any limit whatsoever upon it you suppress something and you gag someone. In practice, however, it was found that if no limitation of these privileges was possible small minorities would abuse them and defeat the will of the majority simply by preventing it from taking action—any action at all. Something had to give, and it has been found that the purposes of democracy will best be served by allowing the right of full and free debate on a proposal to be suspended by a two-thirds vote. The reasoning is that if two thirds of the assembly have made up their minds on a question, we might say, to use the words of the tired toastmaster, "so much has been said, and on the whole so well said, that what remains to be said may as well be left unsaid." A point can be reached where there is little possibility that anything that remains to be said would change enough votes to enable the minority to become the majority and change the outcome.

In the illustration used earlier, the member proposed that debate be closed in ten minutes. This is a good and practical form of the motion, which, appropriately used, would allow both sides to summarize and restate their arguments. There would perhaps be more assurance of the appropriate use of the ten minutes if the proposer moved to limit the debate to "one more five-minute argument from one speaker on each side."

The motion to limit debate may be made in any form the proposer deems good; and, of course, since this is a motion that permits a choice of details, the principle we pointed out earlier applies. In all such instances the assembly, by majority decision, can choose the details. This motion may therefore be amended. The importance of this rule in this instance can be appreciated if you realize that a clever chap might move to limit the debate to one more ten-minute speech from a speaker opposed to the motion, with the view of swaying the assembly by means of a final, heartrending appeal for his side, without opportunity for rebuttal. In this case an amendment should be in order for the sake of justice and fair play.

Lesson 11:

Close Debate

In the previous lesson we learned how debate can be limited. In this lesson we learn how debate can be closed—immediately. The procedure is as follows:

> *Chairman:* Is there any further discussion?
> *Member (after recognition):* I move to close debate (*or I move the previous question.*)
> *Chairman (after second):* It has been moved and seconded to close debate. This motion is undebatable and requires a two-thirds vote. All those in favor of closing debate, raise your hands. All those opposed. The motion to close debate is carried. Discussion is ended. The motion before the house is . . . All those in favor. All opposed. The motion is lost (*or carried*).

The thinking that justified the use of this procedure in a democratic assembly is the same as that for the motion to limit debate. This motion is a bit more drastic because it cuts off debate immediately. It should not be proposed if there is reason to believe that the truly democratic decision on the pending motion might better be reached after some brief additional argument, particularly in the form of a final summary from both sides. It would hardly be fair to propose closing debate on a closely contested proposal immediately after a very lengthy and persuasive appeal or a series of appeals on one side of the question. On the other hand, it is in precisely this situation in which it would most appropriately be used on a very one-sided proposition where a small minority continued to speak its piece at great length, abusing its rights to free debate.

The older and more conventional form of the motion to close debate that you will find listed in *Robert's Rules* is what we have indicated in the example as the motion on the *previous question.* If you are a purist, or if you want to impress people when you want to close debate you may say, "I move the previous question." If you prefer saying what you mean, directly, so that it will be universally understood, you will say "I move to close debate."

You might also use the more modern form for a broader purpose—to bring it into more universal use in American organizations and thereby at the same time let the more confusing and troublesome form die quietly and become archaic. Generally we favor preserving the forms and even the language of the traditional procedure. We indicated specifically in Lesson 9 how the use of the traditional word *table* is good and meaningful when we understand how it came to be from the days of the colonial legislatures, when a proposal "tabled" was returned to the clerk's table. The tradition back of the motion on the previous question, instead of making the term meaningful, only adds to the confusion. You will find the history detailed in *Robert's Rules Revised* (page 117) all the way back to 1604 in England, when the motion was first used. After that it went through a series of changes in our Congress. Today it is simply a motion to close debate and proceed to voting immediately on the pending question.

The effect of the motion to close debate goes beyond merely closing debate as such; it covers debate in the sense of all further consideration of the motion, including amendments or postponing or referring or any other actions that might otherwise be applied to it. The motion to close debate (or the motion on the previous question) is a motion to vote immediately. When it is passed, the chairman proceeds at once to vote the pending motion.

In our illustration at the beginning of this lesson a member proposed closing debate on a proposal or main motion. Debate may also be closed on any other debatable motion, and the motion to close debate is used particularly in the debate on amendments because, as often happens in organizations, the arguments over details grow out of all proportion to their importance.

You can kill several birds with one stone in the situation where a main motion, a primary amendment, and a secondary amendment are pending. You may say, "I move to close debate on both amendments" or go all out and say, "I move to close debate on all pending questions." In this last case, if your motion is carried, the vote on it would be followed by three votes in succession— first on the two amendments and then on the proposal itself.

Lesson 12:
Repeal

We have now completed, in the preceding lessons, the list of the routine motions for transacting the business of a meeting. We have examined the procedure by which a proposal is presented and those by which it may be subjected to treatment of various sorts before it comes finally to a vote and a decision. We have seen, too, how the debate on a motion can be cut short—closed or limited. This is how business is done. We turn now to how business may be undone, for organizations are made up of people and people may change their minds.

There are two ways in which an assembly may reverse a previous action. One is through the motion to reconsider, which brings back the motion for revote. The second is by the direct action to repeal, or rescind, as it is sometimes called. Each procedure has its particular uses, as we shall see. In this lesson we consider the simple and direct one, to repeal.

At any time after a motion has been passed—assuming of course that either considerable time has intervened or that something has happened or been made known that makes the motion to repeal a reasonable one—you may initiate the following dialogue when the assembly is not occupied with other business:

Member (after recognition): I move to repeal the motion passed at our last meeting to send a delegate to our national convention in April.

Chairman (after second): It has been moved and seconded to repeal the motion passed at our last meeting to send a delegate to the national convention in April. Is there any discussion?

Chairman (after discussion): The question is on the repeal of the motion to send a delegate to the April convention. This requires a two-third vote. All those in favor raise your right hands. All those opposed. The motion to repeal is carried. The decision of this assembly to send a delegate to our April convention is reversed.

This motion is treated as an original main motion or proposal with full and free discussion, with the exception that the vote required to repeal will normally be two-thirds of those voting. The two-thirds vote is required in spite of the fact that under *Robert's Rules* we normally carry out the will of the majority. Here the proposal upsets an established decision of the house, and to do this requires two thirds. There is some difference of opinion on whether good democratic procedure might not argue for applying the basic principle of majority rule to undoing business as well as for doing it. The problem with repeal by majority is that in many organizations it would destroy the needed stability and certainty these organizations need to have about decisions made. The business of most organizations is transacted in weekly or monthly meetings, attended in most cases by a small percentage of the total membership. The *quorum,* which is the minimum number that must be present if business is to be legally transacted, may be as low as 20 or 30 or 50 per cent of the total membership. And those who come to the April meeting may be a quite different group than those who came in March. In such a situation a motion passed in March by a very close vote might offer a great temptation for repealing by those who opposed it at the April meeting, if a simple majority could repeal. If we want to feel that what is done is done, we need the stabilizing effect of a two-thirds vote to repeal.

It goes without saying that an organization cannot always properly, and sometimes even possibly, reverse itself. It cannot possibly, by repeal, undo an action that has been taken, and it cannot properly, by repeal, reverse itself on an action that amounts to a contract or word given in good faith.

There is a variation of the motion to repeal that is peculiar to American parliamentary procedure and used to some extent by organizations in this country. This is the motion to *expunge,* which not only repeals the previous action, but expresses strong disapproval of it at the same time. It is used particularly to reverse the action of assemblies in going on record—that is, in the adoption of resolutions as we discussed them in Lesson 3. To expunge has come into use in America from our Congress, where it was used in the administration of President Jackson. In that instance the Senate had passed the resolution censuring him, and later in 1837 Senator Benson introduced into the Senate a motion to expunge this resolution from the record. The motion to expunge is an order to the secretary to inscribe "expunged by order of the assembly" across the original action in the minutes.

Lesson 13:
Reconsider

The simple and direct way to undo a piece of business is to repeal as explained in Lesson 12. There is another way better suited to certain circumstances, through the motion to reconsider.

Member (after recognition): I move to reconsider the motion passed earlier in this meeting to terminate our lease on this clubhouse.
Chairman: Did you vote on the prevailing side?
Member: I did.
Chairman (after second): It has been moved and seconded to reconsider the vote on the motion to terminate our lease on this clubhouse. Is there any discussion? *(after discussion)* All those in favor of reconsidering the question, raise your hands. Those opposed. The vote is affirmative, so the motion again before the house is that we terminate our lease on this clubhouse. Is there any discussion?

As you will note, in the above interchange, the chairman asks the member who proposed to reconsider if he voted on the prevailing side. Only one who has done so may make this motion. This requirement prevents someone on the losing side from using this motion in a useless, desperate, or time-consuming effort on behalf of a cause he has lost. It serves, at the same time, to indicate that there has been a change of opinion in the assembly.

It is the purpose of this motion to provide a procedure for

reopening a question in a situation where new and significant evidence or information might be made available, or some change in the membership present might produce a different majority when the revote is taken. In the illustration the member moving to reconsider may have learned, since voting, that the club was bound by a legally executed lease for another two years. Or it may be that since the vote half a dozen members have come in late. These on a revote might change the result.

The motion to reconsider may be made only by a member who voted on the prevailing side, and it may be made only at the same session as the motion to which it is applied. At your November meeting you may propose to reconsider only motions passed or rejected at that meeting. This is specifically stated in *Robert's Rules* in terms of "only those motions passed or rejected on the same day or the day following," to take care of meetings held in a series such as those at a three- or four-day convention. Essentially it is the purpose of this rule to limit the powers of this motion to undo action primarily to the same majority that took the original action, or to a more representative majority. If it were possible for the December meeting to reconsider the action of a November meeting, the stability needed in decisions made, (provided by the two-thirds vote required for repeal) could be negated through the process of reconsideration, in which we can undo by a majority vote.

Because there are two procedures you can use to undo a motion, you need to know which to use when. If the decision you want reviewed was made at a previous meeting, only repeal is possible. On the other hand, if the motion was passed at the same meeting it would seem that either procedure might be attempted. It is the opinion of some parliamentarians that so long as the motion to reconsider is in order, (that is, at the same session) to reconsider is the only procedure that can properly be used to reverse an assembly. Under some circumstances, to try to *repeal* a piece of business at the same meeting in which it was passed, might be your only recourse. This would be the case if you have not voted on the prevailing side and, therefore, could not make the motion to reconsider. Repeal is also a more direct, a quicker, and an easier procedure. To reconsider requires first a motion to reconsider, then a vote, and then a revote on the motion.

There are two variations of the simple motion to reconsider, available in certain emergency situations. If, near the end of a meeting, for example, a member fears that a quick adjournment may prevent the revote he wants, he can interrupt and "give notice" for a reconsideration:

Member (without waiting for recognition): I move to reconsider the motion to terminate the lease on our clubhouse.
Chairman (after ascertaining that the member voted on the prevailing side, and a second): It has been moved and seconded that we reconsider the motion to terminate our lease. The secretary will make a note of the motion.

In this situation the motion to reconsider will be taken up as soon as the pending business is disposed of. In the second variation the procedure is as follows:

Member: I move to have entered on the minutes a reconsideration of the motion to terminate our lease.
Chairman (after ascertaining that the member voted on the prevailing side, and a second): The secretary will record the notice for a reconsideration of the motion at our next meeting.

This form "to have entered on the minutes the motion to reconsider" prohibits reconsidering *until the next meeting.* This means that because the original motion is now subject to being revoted, it is not duly passed and no action can be taken on it until it is reconsidered and passed again.

This form of the motion to reconsider can obviously be abused; two willful members might theoretically halt action on any proposal. It is justified only in emergency situations—for example, in a very poorly attended meeting in which a definitely unrepresentative majority votes for something that otherwise would never pass. Action on this ought to be held up. This ought to be reconsidered—at the next meeting, in which a more representative vote will be possible. On these and similar grounds it is justified, and only in such circumstances is it in order.

Lesson 14:
Recess and Adjourn

When the time comes in a meeting at which the members are tired and want to take a break, or when they are ready to quit for that session, parliamentary procedure has motions for them. To interrupt the meeting for lunch, for a rest, or for the night, there is the motion to recess.

Member (after recognition): I move we recess until one o'clock.

Chairman (after second): It has been moved and seconded that we recess until one o'clock. All those in favor, raise your right hands. Those opposed. The motion is carried. The meeting is recessed until one o'clock.

This is a *privileged* motion, which means that it may be made even when the assembly is engaged in other business. You must be recognized by the chair to make it, and you cannot interrupt a speaker to do so. When it is made as a privileged motion—that is, when it is proposed when other business is pending—it is not debatable, but it may be amended by changing the specified time. If it is made when no other business is before the house, it is treated as a proposal or main motion and may be debated.

There is a variation of the motion to recess in the form that sets a future time for the break—for example, when a member proposes that the assembly recess in half an hour, or at three o'clock. Because there would be no point in permitting such a proposal to interrupt business, this form is not a privileged motion.

At the time specified for ending a recess, the chairman calls the meeting to order and the assembly takes up where it left off as though there had been no interruption.

Adjourn.   The procedure for ending a meeting is the motion to adjourn. It is quick and direct as follows.

Member (after recognition): I move that we adjourn.

Chairman (after second): It has been moved and seconded that we adjourn. All those in favor. All those opposed. The motion is carried. The meeting is adjourned.

Like the motion to recess, the motion to adjourn is a privileged one. It can be proposed at any time, even though other business is pending. The high privilege accorded these motions is probably based on the viewpoint that whenever an assembly wants to consider quitting it should be given an opportunity. For this reason motions are made undebatable so they can be quickly decided. Either of these motions can be proposed, seconded, and disposed of in ten or fifteen seconds, so there is little harm done if they are raised at any time or even several times in the course of a meeting. Either of the motions may be "renewed"—that is, proposed again after it has failed. They may be renewed after any amount of time has intervened that might reasonably be assumed to change the result in another vote.

There is another motion that is sometimes confused with the motion to adjourn, perhaps because it always appears at the top of the chart in any complete list of motions, with the motion to adjourn. This is what is called the motion "to fix the time to which to adjourn." This is an entirely different proposal. Its purpose is to set the time for the next meeting. As such it has very little use in most organizations. They meet regularly—for example, weekly or monthly—as provided in their constitutions or by-laws, so that the time of the next meeting (the time to which to adjourn) is always fixed. The motion to fix the time to which to adjourn comes into use only in those rare organizations that meet "from time to time" and need to set each succeeding meeting at the preceding one.

Lesson 15:
The Special Emergency Procedures

The diagram in Lesson 4 gives you a picture of what happens when a group follows *Robert's Rules* to conduct its meetings. Actions are in the form of motions, and there are twelve that come into general use. There is the main motion to initiate a proposal, and five subsidiary motions that may be applied to it. There are two motions to restrict debate, two motions to reverse a decision, and two to end meetings. It is the use of these, as we have illustrated them in the preceding lessons, that makes parliamentary practice what it is.

For the normal and routine transaction of the business in most voluntary societies these will suffice. But sometimes in meetings things will not be normal. Sometimes the routine will be upset. When this happens special procedures will be needed by which the members can take steps to ensure that the rules are properly enforced, that those present are reasonably comfortable, or at least unharrassed and unmolested, that they have access to pertinent information as it is needed, that they are not "put upon" by a dictatorial chairman, and that they are not obliged to suffer unnecessarily from the follies of intemperate or unwise fellow members.

Parliamentary procedure provides a series of procedures, usually listed in the conventional charts as the "incidental motions," through which, if you know how to use them, you can protect your rights and privileges as they might be interfered with in each of the ways we have mentioned above. We call these the *special emergency procedures*—*special* because they are out of the routine handling of business, *emergency* because to a great extent each comes into use in what is at least a limited emergency situation, and *procedures* because they are not motions in the sense that they are not introduced in the form "I move" and they are not handled as motions.

The conventional terms for these are the following:
1. Point of order.
2. Appeal from the decision of the chair.
3. Parliamentary inquiry.
4. Request for information.
5. Point of privilege.
6. Objection to consideration.

A specific and typical use of each of these can be quickly illustrated. If the speaker who has the floor is wandering from the subject, you can interrupt with a point of order to call the attention of the chairman to this infraction of the rules. If you are seated in the rear of the room, those about you are making too much noise, and you cannot hear, you can interrupt, "rising to a point of privilege," to insist that the situation be remedied.

If you have a question concerning proper procedure—on how something should be done, or might be done, or whether it can be done—you raise a "parliamentary inquiry." If at a particular juncture it is important to know when a guest lecturer is coming, or how much money is in the treasury, or whether the speaker knows what his proposal will cost, you rise to a "request for information." If you feel the presiding officer has made an incorrect ruling or an unfair decision, you "appeal from the decision of the chair." When one of your less discreet fellow members presents a proposal that is embarrassing, intemperate, or unwise, you "object to its consideration."

Lesson 16:
Point of Order

At any point in a meeting when you believe that some rule is not properly enforced or for any reason you believe that a member or the assembly is proceeding improperly, you may call the attention of the presiding officer to the fact. To do this you take the part of the member in the following dialogue, without waiting for recognition from the chair, and interrupting the speaker if necessary:

Member: Mr. Chairman, I rise to a point of order, (*or simply* Point of order.)
Chairman: What is your point? (*or* State your point.)
Member: We have a proposal before the house to send a delegate to our national convention, but the immediately pending motion is one to pay only his traveling expenses. The speaker who has the floor is discussing the question whether we should send a delegate and not the amendment for paying the traveling expenses. I feel that his discussion is therefore out of order at this time.
Chairman: Your point of order is well taken. The speaker will please confine his remarks to the immediately pending question, which is on the amendment. The speaker may continue.

It is the duty of the chairman to see to it that all of the rules are observed, that there is good order in the hall, and that the members behave with decorum. Inevitably there will be differences of opinion. Members may differ with the chair about an interpretation of the rules. At other times there will be infractions that the chair may not notice.

In serious cases of the violation of good order by a speaker, where it involves such indecorum in debate as offensive language, disrespect to the presiding officer, or to other members, a member, instead of rising to a point of order, may himself call another to order. He may rise and interrupt by saying the following:

Member: Mr. Chairman, I call the gentleman to order.
Chairman: The point is well taken. The chair rules the speaker out of order and he is directed to take his seat.

This would be the more serious result of your direct calling of the speaker to order. Instead of ruling the speaker out of order and off the floor, as in the above instance, the chairman might simply "call him to order" reminding him that he must cease and desist this sort of attack and allowing him to continue.

Because a point of order is quick and easy to make, and because it is rather difficult in a specific instance to point an accusing finger at a member who misuses it, this procedure is probably the most abused and misused of all parliamentary devices, particularly in less experienced assemblies and in younger student groups. Perhaps it is abused because it is so great a temptation to exhibitionism; through it, a nameless and faceless one, otherwise destined to go unnoticed and lost among a hundred or a thousand members, can by simply rising and bellowing "point of order" stop everything and have all eyes centered upon him —even if he has nothing of consequence to say. A point of order should be, as we have classified it, a special emergency procedure to stop or to prevent an infraction of the rules of some consequence. It should not be used on little irregularities or on technical points of no consequence. In an assembly unfamiliar with the technicalities of procedure there is no quicker way for a member to make both himself and proper parliamentary procedure unpopular than to frequently and pointlessly interject "Point of order!"

Lesson 17:
Appeal from the Decision of the Chair

It is the duty of the presiding officer to enforce the rules. To do this he must interpret the rules and apply them in specific instances, and generally meetings will be run best if we leave the task to him. This will be particularly true if he is sufficiently competent to do a good job and (partly as a result of his competence) if we have confidence in his ability and his objectivity and fairness. Because presiding officers do not always measure up to these standards and because, even when they do, they may sometimes make mistakes, we have a potential parliamentary problem. The solution is provided in the second of our special emergency procedures, an appeal from the decision of the chair, which goes like this:

Chairman: The chair rules this amendment out of order on the ground that it is not germane to the main motion.

Member (without waiting for recognition): I appeal from the decision of the chair.

Chairman (after second): The decision of the chair has been appealed from. Will those who believe the amendment is germane and would sustain the ruling of the chair, raise your hands. Those opposed. The decision of the chair is overruled.

The first principle to guide you in the use of this motion is that it is in the interests of the whole assembly that you take a stand against the chairman when you believe he is wrong. It is your duty to make use of this procedure when it is needed. Corollary to this is the principle that, although generally we will abide by *Robert's Rules* as our presiding officer interprets them, when a question arises, as it will only on difficult and doubtful rulings (close ones), it is best to appeal to the assembly for a decision and abide by the judgment of the majority.

An appeal must be made immediately after the decision of the chair has been made, and if any other business or debate has intervened it is too late. This is why no recognition is needed to appeal and a member may interrupt, even when another member has the floor.

Members may sometimes feel a natural reluctance to appeal, on the ground that either it involves a kind of presumptuous criticism of the chair's competence or that it is a personal attack on the chairman. It is, rather, a vital part of the democratic process in parliamentary procedure because it is the only way in which we can achieve some discussion of the question and hear both sides. Ordinarily, decisions of the chairman are undebatable. This means that he has no opportunity to state his reasons for his viewpoint, and neither does a member who differs. The opportunity for debate is opened by the appeal. It does not permit full-scale debate, but it does permit limited explanations. The member may state his reasons for making the appeal and the chairman may in turn explain his decision. For this reason most chairmen will welcome an appeal of any decisions that arouse some difference of opinion, and perhaps also because the appeal relieves them of responsibility for the final decision, throwing it to the assembly.

Instances for the use of appeal may arise at almost any time in a meeting, but they will arise most often after a member has raised a point of order and it has been denied by the presiding officer. It is for this reason that we have listed this procedure following point of order in our list, and it is for this reason that we have placed this lesson following our consideration of point of order. A typical exchange would go like this:

Member (after recognition): The motion before the house is that we invite the Democratic candidate for mayor to the April meeting. I move to amend the motion by adding the words "and that we invite the Republican candidate to the May meeting."

Chairman (after second): It has been moved and seconded that we amend this proposal by adding the words, "and that we invite the Republican candidate to the May meeting." Is there any discussion?

Member (without recognition): Point of order.

Chairman: What is your point?

Member: I believe that this amendment is out of order. To propose to invite the Republican candidate is a new and different question, and the amendment is therefore not germane.

Chairman: The chairman rules that the amendment is germane. Is there any further discussion?

Member: I appeal from the decision of the chair.

Chairman: The decision of the chair has been appealed. All those in favor of sustaining the ruling of the chair in the ruling that the amendment is germane, raise your hands. Those opposed. The vote is affirmative. The ruling of the chair stands as the decision of the assembly. Is there any further discussion on the amendment to add the words, "and that the Republican candidate be invited to the May meeting"?

There is obviously a potential danger in the availability of this procedure to a willful majority in that they could vote to sustain an appeal contrary to a good and proper ruling by the chairman and in effect nullify the constitutional provision requiring them to follow the *Rules.* Parliamentary procedure accepts this potential danger as a better alternative than that of being without some recourse against an improper ruling by a dictatorial chairman. The safeguard against the potential danger is in the assumption that assemblies will abide by the *Rules* when it is clear what the rules are and the realization that to pervert the *Rules* is to do so at their peril. To pervert them is to destroy the foundations of the democratic institution in which they are functioning. In cases where it is not clear what the rules are—that is, on the moot points—the assumption is that ultimately it is best to let the assembly decide what the interpretation of the rule should be.

Lesson 18:
Parliamentary Inquiry

Democracy in meetings is not served if a member, through some lack of knowledge of a complexity of procedure, is prevented from doing what he believes ought to be done. Parliamentary practice recognizes the importance of this truth in a regular procedure duly established and of long tradition called the *parliamentary inquiry.* Its purpose and usefulness are illustrated in the following dialogue, which might take place in a meeting after some member had presented a proposal to invite the Mayor to speak at the next regular meeting and some member felt it might be a nice gesture to extend an invitation at the same time to the members of the City Council. He is not quite sure how to go about it, but he has gumption enough to ask.

Member: Mr. Chairman. I rise to a parliamentary inquiry.
Chairman: What is your question?
Member: I believe that if we invite the Mayor to speak at our April meeting we should also invite the members of the City Council to be our guests at that time, and my question is whether or not an amendment to the original motion to this effect would be in order at this time.
Chairman: The chair believes that such an amendment would be proper at this time.
Member: Thank you, Mr. Chairman. I move to amend the motion before the house by adding the words, "and that the members of the City Council be invited as our guests."

You use a parliamentary inquiry to get *parliamentary* information. You use it to inquire how the *Rules* apply to something that is being done or has been done. It furnishes, in many instances, a nice substitute for the blunt and sometimes resented point of order. In more polite societies there is obvious courtesy and real finesse in inquiring respectfully whether the remarks of a speaker might not be deemed out of order—finesse that is lacking in a point of order.

The parliamentary inquiry must be concerned with the rules or a matter of procedure. If it is other information you need you use *request for information,* as we shall see in the next lesson. You may rise to a parliamentary inquiry at any time, interrupting a speaker if necessary, but only if the answer is essential at the time. An example of a proper instance is to interrupt a speaker who is going beyond his time limit, to ask the presiding officer if he has not exhausted his time.

Lesson 19:
Request for Information

How to Get the Facts and Figures. Sometimes in meetings certain facts or a particular piece of information may be essential, here and now, if the assembly is to proceed intelligently. A

speaker arguing for a proposal that costs money may be wasting
your time and his if he is misinformed and the assembly does
not know that there are no funds available. As meetings progress
it is necessary sometimes to know how much money is in the
treasury, when the speaker (or the coffee) is coming, or possibly
when the janitor is going to turn out the lights. Common sense
dictates that we need a way to get such pieces of information.
Speaking more broadly, because the members of a democratic
organization have a right to be informed, there ought to be a
procedure that will elicit information formally and immediately
when it is essential to the discussion. In the previous lesson we
considered how information on how to proceed may be obtained
through parliamentary inquiry. Our concern here is how to get
all other kinds of information (not procedural). The method is
as follows:

> *Member (interrupting if necessary):* Mr. Chairman, I rise for in-
> formation.
> *Chairman:* What is your question?
> *Member:* At what time is the dean scheduled to arrive?
> *Chairman:* We have invited the dean to speak to us at 8:00.

If we take as assumptions that the dean will be on time and
that when he comes he is not to be kept waiting, and if we
assume also that this fact is critical to certain business to be
transacted before he arrives, then we have an example of the
proper use and value of "rising to a request for information."
In this case it is a piece of information that can be provided by
the chairman. At other times a member may wish to question
the speaker who has the floor; and because this may be aimed
more at putting him on the spot by forcing him to face up to an
ugly fact than at obtaining needed information, there must be
some limitations. If there were not, speakers could be unfairly
and continuously heckled. When a speaker has the floor, he may
use his time as he chooses, and this may not include answering
questions at the will of the members. You may rise to a point
of information to ask the speaker a question, but you may not
get an answer, as the following indicates:

Member (interrupting): I rise to a point of information.
Chairman: What is your question?
Member: I would like to ask the speaker a question.
Chairman: Will the speaker yield to a question?
Speaker: I prefer not to yield until I have finished my remarks. If any questions remain at that time, I'll be happy to answer them.
Chairman: The speaker will not yield the floor for questions. He may continue.

You will note that the speaker does not refuse bluntly to answer the question, but suggests that it might be better to wait until he has finished, when the question may no longer be necessary. He also indicates at the same time that he does not intend to yield for questions until he is finished, thereby serving notice that he does not intend to be bothered or heckled by further questions. There may be times, however, when it is in the interests of the assembly that a speaker be forced at once to answer a question. If this were true in the above instance, the member might push the matter further after the speaker has indicated he will not yield by rising to a point of privilege (or a point of order) attempting to make the question a matter that is vital to the privileges and rights of the assembly at this point, insisting the information be given before the speaker is allowed to continue. Matters of privilege will be taken up in the next lesson.

Lesson 20:
Point of Privilege

In the beginning of this section on the special procedures made available to the member to protect his rights and privileges, it was pointed out that among these is the right to conditions in the meeting suitable to getting the job done. You have a right to be reasonably comfortable, to hear, to be free from harassments and disturbances. At the same time you have a duty to protect your fellow members and the assembly as a whole from unsatisfactory conditions. You do this with the point of privilege:

Member (*interrupting if necessary*): Mr. Chairman, I rise to a point of privilege.

Chairman: What is your point? (*or* Please state your point.)

Member: It is impossible for those of us in the rear of the hall to hear the speaker.

Chairman: Your privilege is granted. Will someone please turn up the loudspeaker system? Will the speaker please move closer to the microphone, and continue?

In this case the point of privilege might properly be considered of sufficient urgency to interrupt the speaker and to be granted immediately by the presiding officer. A point of privilege relating to the comfort of the members such as heating, lighting, or ventilation might more properly be considered of an urgency sufficient to interrupt business, but not to interrupt the speaker. In such an instance, a member will rise to a point of privilege immediately after a speaker has concluded. If the chair has already recognized some other member for discussion, the fact that a point of privilege has been raised will cause the presiding officer to permit it to be considered at once. The speaker who has been recognized will await the settlement of the matter before he goes ahead with his discussion. If the only urgency about a matter of privilege rests in the fact that it ought to be considered ahead of other matters on the agenda or that routine procedure might prevent its being considered before the meeting adjourned, then it should not interrupt a speaker and it need not interrupt another piece of business. It may wait until a pending question has been disposed of and then, even after the chairman has placed before the house another new piece of business, you may rise and inform the chairman that you have a point of privilege to bring to the attention of the assembly. This may even be a formal proposal, a new main motion—for example,

Member (*without waiting for recognition*): Mr. Chairman, I rise to a point of privilege.

Chairman: State your point.

Member: As a matter of privilege, I move that reporters and photographers be barred from the remainder of this meeting.

Chairman: Your privilege is granted. Is there a second to the motion? . . . It has been moved and seconded that reporters and photographers be barred from the remainder of the meeting. Is there any discussion?

In this instance we might assume the member feels that reporters and photographers should be barred because they are disturbing the meeting or because there is business ahead that can better be discussed with some privacy and is not for public consumption. It is possible to conceive how this same situation might arise and become critical in the midst of the consideration of a piece of business or even as a speaker held the floor. In such circumstances a member should use the point of privilege to give the motion to bar reporters at once the very high privilege of being considered immediately.

The procedure just considered, by which a proposal or a motion may be made a privileged one, has led to some confusion through the use of such terms as *questions of privilege, privileged questions,* and *privileged motions.* In Lesson 14 we considered the "privileged motions" to recess and to adjourn, called privileged because they take precedence over all other motions. Because motions are questions (for the assembly to answer) it is reasonable to designate recess and adjourn *privileged questions.* To distinguish it from these, the procedure that is the subject of this lesson can best be called *point of privilege,* and when it is used the member should say he rises to a *point* of privilege rather than to a *question* of privilege.

Lesson 21:
Objection to Consideration

Assemblies sometimes need to be protected from the follies of their members—particularly ill-advised, embarrassing, time-wasting, intemperate, or just plain stupid proposals that will sometimes come up. Consider the following dialogue, which might take place in what might normally be a polite and reasonable society.

Chairman: Is there any further business?

Member (after recognition): I move that we have an immediate investigation of our treasurer's accounts.

Chairman (after second): It has been moved and seconded that we have an immediate investigation of our treasurer's accounts. Is there any discussion?

Member (after recognition): There are rumors going around that our treasurer has been careless with our accounts. Certain members who shall be nameless have told me that they are suspicious . . .

Member (interrupting): I object to the consideration of this question.

Chairman: Objection has been raised to the consideration of this question. All those in favor of considering the question, raise your hands. All those opposed. Since more than two thirds sustain the objection, the question cannot be considered and it is dropped. Is there any other new business?

If we assume in this instance that the proposer of this investigation (1) is a traditional troublemaker, (2) has a grudge against the treasurer, and (3) is bent upon making a nasty and intemperate speech that at best should never be delivered, we have a good example of the utility and effectiveness of the special procedure that is the subject of this lesson.

There are other ways to kill a motion—by postponing indefinitely or closing debate and voting it down—but objection to consideration is "sudden death," cutting off even the opportunity for any initial discussion of the proposal. It is obvious that if this procedure is to be effective it must be permitted to interrupt the speaker, as in the instance just described. There would not be much point to it if we could not interrupt and shut off that first member until after he had come to the end of some ill-advised and intemperate remarks.

Because this is a drastic sort of procedure, certain limitations are placed upon it by the *Rules* and others must, in practice, be exercised in connection with it. The procedure is drastic in that it makes possible the violation of the right of any member to introduce any proposal that he considers appropriate if he can get the support of another member who will second his motion. The first limitation imposed by the *Rules* is that at least a two-thirds vote is required immediately (without discussion and on the face of it) to sustain the objection—that is, to refuse to consider the question. The second limitation is that the objection must be raised immediately after the question has been proposed. It is out of order after the discussion has progressed or debate has arisen. There is a practical limitation that will come from the good sense of members realizing that if they tolerate the misuse of this procedure to prevent the consideration of proposals of a minority they are encouraging a practice that can, in their organization, mean the end of the democratic right of a minority to be heard. Your criteria for raising an objection to consideration should be, not so much that the proposal deserves to be defeated, but rather that it should not be considered—that the discussion of it will be harmful, objectionable, embarrassing, contentious, or merely useless. When these things are true, objection to consideration is a good and useful procedure, well suited to the best purposes of a democratic society.

PART II

Presiding as Chairman

MONARCHY had one advantage over democracy. The man who was to be its leader, to preside over its affairs, was usually told about it soon enough so that he could spend the early part of a lifetime learning to handle the job. In the democratic order of things it is not uncommon to elect a president at a Monday evening meeting and expect him to come prepared to take over at the meeting on the following Monday.

This potential problem in the democratic way of doing things enables us to say proudly that "any man can be president," but if we are going to be worthy of what the saying implies, then each of us has a duty to prepare himself for the day he may be elected.

Elected or not, any member will find the preparation useful; whatever he can learn of the knowledge a chairman must have will make any member a more effective one. It will also likely get him elected, because knowing how to preside is the best qualification for office and candidates so qualified are hard to find and seldom successfully opposed.

Your preparation to preside is already well on its way if you have learned the lessons in Part I of this book. You have more than completed your "basic training" to serve as an officer. You have yet to learn something of what may aptly be called the art of presiding—how to direct the procedure—and the science of presiding—how to enforce the rules. Finally you need to know how to run a meeting—to handle the typical agenda on order of business. These are your agenda in the next three lessons.

Lesson 22:
The Art of Presiding—Directing the Procedure

Good chairmanship involves the art of directing the procedure and the science of enforcing the rules. The rules are guide
lines that must be followed if democratic principles are to be
carried out. The procedure, on the other hand, is the method
and form by which the operation is carried on, including (1) the
physical arrangement in a meeting with the chairman at the
center of things and in charge, (2) the motion process, (3) the
core procedure, and (4) the structural arrangement of the process
from proposal through discussion, subsidiary motions, possible
interruptions by the special procedures, and finally the decision
by vote. The rules make democracy prevail. The procedure provides order. Combined they provide ordered democracy. That is
what parliamentary procedure is for.

The chairman enforces the rules because they are laws his
organization has agreed to observe when its constitution was
adopted. The chairman follows the procedure for the sake of
order, and this gives him a special concern for good procedure.
It is part of his job to maintain order, and he has an impossible
job if he does not.

Order begins in a meeting when the chairman pounds the
table with his gavel and says, "Will the meeting please come to
order?" This is both a signal and a directive that the attention
of the assembly should now be directed to him. At this point
he assumes the responsibility given him when he was elected—
that of presiding or taking charge of the meeting. This gives
meaning to the first element of parliamentary procedure—the
physical arrangement of the presiding officer up front, at the
focus of the attention of the assembly, in charge, and directing
the proceedings.

The position of the presiding officer entails a particular kind
of leadership and direction that is best understood in comparison
with other types of leaders. At one end of the scale there is the
military general, who calls a meeting of his men and gives his
battle orders; the most that might come from them is a response

to his final "Any questions, gentlemen?" Next there is the corpora-
tion president or superintendent or "boss," who calls in his vice-
presidents or divisional managers or foremen and outlines his
policies. He may ask for questions, and usually beyond this ask
for and encourage comment and discussion, listening to them
with the view of modifying his policies on the basis of what
he considers good advice. Then there is the "Chairman of the
Board" who assembles his directors and operates largely with
their advice and consent. The planning, projecting, and decision-
making may be largely his, but he may generally try to fit his
decisions to the consensus of the group. For those who have
studied the duties of the group discussion leader, as these are
described in contemporary discussion theory, a comparison will
be profitable. A group leader might be called the chairman, except he does not preside in the sense that he sits out front. His
position in relation to the other members is a completely democratic one. He can participate and influence the outcome of the
deliberations, and he has no particular prerogatives in the nature
of rules to enforce or a procedure to direct. He is one with them
in the group process. In this scale of leadership from the general
to the discussion leader the parliamentary chairman comes at the
end. He neither gives orders, plans policies, asks advice, nor even
gives it. He does not influence the decision as the group discussion leader does. He leads only in the sense of showing the way,
through the enforcement of the rules and the directing of the
procedure, to how decisions by the will of the majority can best
be reached.

The chairman takes charge when he calls the meeting to order.
The secret of keeping order is to stay in charge, always. This
means that all of the discussion and all of the transactions must
be directed to him and take place through him. In practice this
makes the first procedural concern of the chairman the proper
use of the core procedure as it was presented in Lesson 2. Each
of the steps involved in that procedure assists the chair in doing
his job. By insisting that a member be recognized before he
speaks, he ensures that one person at a time has the floor and
avoids the bedlam of many speaking at once and the disorder of
any two or three engaging in a personal interchange. By insisting

on the formal presentation of a motion before any explanatory or argumentative speech making is permitted to introduce it, he has a basis, first for judging whether the subject is an appropriate and proper one, suited to the purposes of the meeting, and second, a basis of ruling whether or not the discussion on it is in order—that is, germane.

After the motion has been made and seconded the chairman restates it. This procedure serves several purposes. If the motion was poorly worded originally he may, with the cooperation and consent of the proposer, develop a better wording. This restatement of the motion by the chairman is the official wording, and the one that goes into the minutes. The restatement helps to fix in the minds of the members exactly what is before the house. And the restatement is due notice that all is clear now for the discussion. A presiding officer's reputation for skill and effectiveness will depend on the ease and rapidity with which he carries out his duties. In turn, his ease and rapidity will depend on how well he knows the formulas for meeting each situation. Command of the appropriate language comes with practice. Until practice has made perfect the inexperienced presiding officer may find it useful to read aloud and even drill himself in the chairman's lines. These lines may vary a bit to suit the practices of some organizations, but there is merit in following them rather closely, because they are the universal language of parliamentary procedure.

The real art of the chairman is exercised in controlling the discussion and debate within the limits proper procedure prescribes for them. All that is said is by his leave, on his judgment that it is in order. His guiding principle here is that the discussion must be germane to the immediately pending question. That discussion is germane which may be judged useful to making the decision immediately ahead. The application of this principle may lead to some difference of opinion—for example, from the garrulous member who is rehashing for the third time the reasons why he is against a motion. He is out of order, and the chair may so remind him. In this instance, however, it may be better to be president than right, so the wise president enforces the rule of what is germane with some latitude and a great respect

for freedom of speech. This is not to say that an occasional reminder of this rule to American assemblies would not be a great
help to expediting better procedure. The chairman can give
such a reminder if, instead of using the usual form of ruling
discussion out of order by saying that it is "not germane," he will
rule it out of order because it is "not contributing to the reaching
of a decision by this assembly."

In addition to keeping the discussion useful to the immediate
purposes of the assembly, it is the chair's responsibility to see
to it that it suits both the principles of good logic and of democracy. Good logic argues that the proposer of a motion should
have a prior right to the floor—to open the discussion. Logic
requires this because in this speech we assume we will learn
more about this proposal than can be stated in the motion itself.
Generally the chair also recognizes the privilege of the proposer
to speak last, to close the discussion, just before the vote.

Keeping the discussion democratic involves, first, equality of
opportunity and then fairness. Equality of opportunity argues
that the chairman will try to give each member an opportunity
to contribute. If two speakers want the floor, the one who has not
spoken previously on the proposal should be recognized before
the one who has. Fairness argues that the chairman will not show
bias in recognizing speakers. When the assembly tends to divide
itself for and against a proposition, he will alternate with speakers
for and against, insofar as this is feasible. Finally, he will imple-
ment what good procedure demands for full and free debate,
first, by avoiding rushing the vote and thereby cutting off contributions that would be made if opportunity were given for
them. He will avoid the use of the sometimes suggested procedure of asking the assembly, "Are you ready for the question?"
thereby encouraging a clamorous "yes" from the majority and
thereby discouraging contributions that otherwise might be forthcoming. Debate is properly closed only by asking, "Is there any
further discussion?" and waiting to be sure there is none.

In addition to conducting properly the discussion and debate
that takes place in the meetings at which he presides, the chairman must handle whatever else the somewhat loosely used term
discussion includes. In addition to being discussed, a motion

may be dropped, amended, referred to a committee, postponed to another time, or tabled. Conducting a meeting or presiding therefore may involve the handling of all of these motions. In the preceding lessons each of these was illustrated as it is used by a member. For the chairman there is more to be mastered if these motions are to be effectively handled by him.

Postpone Indefinitely.   In Lesson 5 on the motion to postpone indefinitely the point was made that this motion is unique in that the discussion of it permits a discussion of the merits of the main motion to which it is applied. If, for example, after it has been moved to postpone indefinitely a proposal to invite the reform candidate for mayor to speak at the next meeting, a member proceeds to deliver his strong opinions against the candidate, you cannot call him to order on the ground that he is not discussing the immediately pending question (postpone indefinitely) if his remarks are germane to the main question, which is whether or not the candidate for mayor should be invited.

Amend.   There are two procedural problems of particular concern to the presiding officer in the handling of motions to amend. Both have to do with what is, and what is not germane. The first is whether or not the amendment itself is germane. The second is whether or not the discussion on it is germane. The criteria by which the member decides whether or not any amendment is germane were considered in Lesson 6. The rule the chairman should remember is that a member may move to *change* a proposal but he cannot move to *interchange* it with another. If, for example, the main motion is "that we buy the chairman a new gavel" and a member moved to amend by striking out the words "chairman a new gavel" and substituting "a new record book for the secretary" this is to interchange one proposal for another and should be ruled out of order. If, on the other hand, a member moved to amend the original motion by striking out the word "new" and substituting the word "used" this would be changing the proposal and therefore in order.

It is clear enough how the rules should be applied in the example we have given, but sometimes it is not so easy. If, in the above instance, the member interested in getting a new record book for the secretary had moved instead to amend by adding the words "and the secretary a new record book" after "gavel," does this make the motion a different proposal, or is this a modification? For the chairman there is an easy way out of the difficulty. It is a proper one that he may use in any problem situation—one that not only takes him "off the hook" but is also genuinely democratic. He puts the question to the assembly by the following procedure:

Chairman: The chair is in doubt, so the question will be decided by the assembly. All those who feel the amendment is in order, raise your hands. Those opposed. The vote is negative. The house rules that the amendment is not germane at this time, so the motion to amend is dropped. Is there any further discussion on the motion to buy the chairman a new gavel?

If the chairman wishes to rule on the amendment, his decision is based on the principle that he believes it makes procedural sense to discuss these two proposals as one, made up of two related items. On the other hand, if he feels that these are two separate items, best discussed and voted separately, then he should rule the amendment out of order. A member objecting to voting on a "double" motion may call for "a division of the question" and if he does, it must be divided.

The rule against interchanging one thing for another applies equally when the chairman is faced with a proposal to modify an amendment—that is, an amendment to an amendment. This must be germane—that is, it must suggest a change in the amendment, but it cannot interchange it with another. Returning to the situation above, with the motion to "buy the chairman a new gavel" pending, and the proposed amendment to substitute "used" for "new," it would be in order to amend the amendment by adding the word "mahogany" after "used." This is a modification of the amendment, a suggestion from a member who has some particular reason for believing that, if a used gavel is to be purchased, it should be made of mahogany. On the other hand, to propose at this point to amend by substituting the word "mahogany" for "used" would be out of order because this is interchanging the amendment (interchanging "mahogany" for "used") and not modifying it.

As was pointed out above, the chairman has first the problem of assuring that the proposed amendment is germane. His next problem is to keep the discussion germane to the amendments. There is the basic rule in parliamentary procedure that the discussion must always relate to the immediately pending question. The immediately pending question is the last motion made (if it is accepted)—the immediate question being considered. For example, in the situation above there is the main motion to buy a new gavel, the primary amendment to make it a used one, and the secondary amendment proposing that the used one be of mahogany. At this point the immediately pending question is, "If it is to be a used one, should it be mahogany?" All discussion of the main question to buy or not to buy and all discussion of "used" or "not used" is out of order at this point. If the secondary amendment is passed, the question then becomes, "If we buy the gavel should it be used mahogany?" or "should it be new?" If this amendment is passed (as amended), the question before the house now becomes the original motion amended: "that we buy the chairman a used mahogany gavel."

The prospect of keeping these things straight may frighten a prospective chairman, but he can take comfort in the thought that in the practical affairs of most organizations, the procedure seldom reaches this stage of complexity. Then too, he should realize that he has the privilege of insisting on the assistance both of the secretary and the membership in keeping things straight. The secretary should be recording these proposals as they come and be ready to read them off for the chairman. From the members he should insist on clear, precise, and proper forms of amendment, most particularly with respect to the use of what we call the "editing" process. This was explained in detail in Lesson 6 as the proper method for members to follow. The wise chairman will insist that they follow it.

In return for insisting upon precision and clarity from the membership, it is to be expected that the chairman will respond in kind. He will do this most particularly by giving precise statements of what is pending at any time. Precise means saying just enough, avoiding saying too much. When the secondary amendment is pending he will say no more than that "the question is whether or not we should insert 'mahogany' after 'used'," both when he states the question for discussion so the assembly will know exactly what is being discussed, and when he states it for the vote, so they will know what they are voting for. If the secondary amendment is carried he will say, "The question now is whether or not we should substitute 'used mahogany' for 'new' before 'gavel' in the original motion." And finally if this amended amendment is passed, he will say:

Chairman: The question now before the house is the original motion as amended: that we should buy the chairman a used mahogany gavel. Is there any discussion?

Because the amendment procedure can be extremely useful in achieving both democracy and efficiency in a group, the chairman should be both helpful and encouraging to his membership in the proper use of amendments. This may take the form both of direct suggestions on how a member may best achieve his purposes in modifying a motion and also in the direction of helping to make the procedure as clear and simple as possible. A particular way in which the chairman can be helpful is in connection with the process by which a member who has proposed a motion may accept an amendment as this was explained in Lesson 6. When an amendment is proposed that is favorable to the original motion—and most are—a chairman might immediately inquire whether or not the proposer would like to accept the amendment. In most cases he will accept it, and this will expedite the procedure, eliminate the speech in favor of the amendment, avoid discussion on it, and possibly a debate.

One final problem remains with respect to directing proper procedure in the handling of amendments by the chairman. This is in connection with the process of filling blanks. Essentially he must arrive at a point where he gets a majority vote for one of the alternatives. If it is names or things he usually asks for suggestions and lists them in the order they are received from the floor.

When all are listed, by show of hands, he finds one with majority support. If a sum or amount is involved as in the case of a motion to donate "a blank sum" to the United Fund, he asks for suggestions and lists the amounts from the highest to the lowest and then takes a show of hands in that order. In this case, if the assembly is voting logically, he will get a majority somewhere on his way down through the list because each of those voting for one of the greater sums will usually vote again for the sum that is next lower.

The normal procedure (and perhaps the more proper one) in filing a blank is to fill the blank first—that is select the name, color, or sum—and then vote on the motion. It is done this way because a proposal is first perfected or completed and then voted upon. To do otherwise is to vote "a blank check," so to speak. In certain instances, however, it is possible that the best interests of an organization might be reached by passing the main motion first, with the blank in it, and filling the blank afterwards. For example, in a proposal to send a delegate on a very pleasant trip to a convention there may be a very sharp difference of opinion on whether it should be Mr. Smith or Mr. Jones. The decision on the basic question may best be reached by leaving these personalities out of it by deciding the basic question first. This will be done if the main motion is voted first and the blank is filled afterwards. Here again the chairman, exercising the sort of intelligent leadership that should be his general practice, might well direct the assembly in the best procedure by judicious suggestion.

Sometimes a member in his attempt to amend a motion will find it easier to strike out all the words after "I move that" and substitute an entirely new wording. This is called a substitute motion and can be illustrated in the situation in which the original motion was that "we invite our Senior Senator to speak at our annual dinner," and the member proceeds as follows:

Member: I move to amend the motion by striking out all the words after "I move that" and substituting "we appoint a committee to select and engage a speaker for our annual meeting."

The normal procedure here should present no particular problem for the chairman. The discussion would be on the relative merits of the two propositions and then the vote on whether or not the second should replace the first as the motion before the house. There is a problem, however, in that no opportunity is provided for modifying (perfecting) the original motion. It is possible that the members might find a great deal more merit in the original suggestion if it were amended by striking out the word "we" and substituting "our chairman" so that the proposal would be to have the chairman invite the Senior Senator to speak. In such instances the chairman may provide the assembly an opportunity for amending both the original motion and the substitute before it votes on which to choose. Here again is an opportunity for the presiding officer to exercise his prime function of directing the procedure to the fullest achievement of the best possible decision by his assembly.

Refer to a Committee.   Achieving the best procedure in connection with the motion to refer is a matter of getting the best people on the committee. There are three ways these may be chosen. The member may name them in his motion (saying that this motion be referred "to a committee of three, consisting of Jones, Smith, and Brown"), they may be elected from the house, or they may be appointed by the chair. If the job to be done by the committee is such that it can make particular use of the competence, experience, or connections of certain members who can be named by the proposer of the motion, this is good. If the original proposal has been a very controversial one leading to a divided assembly, the assembly may insist and the chairman may happily agree that the committee should be chosen by the assembly. In most other situations and as a general practice the members of a committee are best appointed by the presiding officer. He is likely to know the qualifications of the various members best—not only their competence to carry out the task, but perhaps more particularly their willingness to get it done on schedule. For this reason, in many organizations it is standard practice for the chairman to appoint committees. Where it is not, the chairman may encourage the practice by saying, after the general motion to refer has been adopted, that if there is no objection the chairman will appoint the committee.

Postpone Definitely. In the matter of the motion to postpone definitely the prime concern of the presiding officer is getting postponed motions properly to the floor for consideration when the time set arrives. Motions postponed "until the next meeting" would be considered under "old" or "unfinished" business. Here the chairman will be reminded that they are on the agenda at the outset of the meeting when the secretary reads the minutes. When "unfinished business" is reached, he can turn to the secretary and ask for a reading of the first item of postponed business. Items assigned to a particular hour are a slightly different problem. They are "orders of the day"—either "general" or "special." A general order is the result of the ordinary procedure of postponing a piece of business to a certain time by majority vote. If the time set is three o'clock, the postponed business is taken up either at three, or if a piece of business is in progress, as soon as that business is completed. A special order is so made by specific statement to that effect in the motion to postpone definitely; it is passed by a two-thirds vote. A special order differs from a general one in that it interrupts whatever business may be in progress when the time comes, unless, of course, another special order happens to be in progress at that time. The presiding officer handles general and special orders competing for time by applying these rules:

1. General orders always yield to special orders.
2. A special order created later yields to one created earlier.
3. A general order set for a later time always yields to one set for an earlier time.

In practice these rules mean that a special order is always taken up when its time comes, unless it comes into conflict with another special order created earlier. General orders never interrupt, and, where they come in conflict with each other they are taken up chronologically according to the time to which they were assigned. These rules are, on first reading, somewhat complex, but it may be added that they are supplied for solving a sort of complexity that will very rarely occur in the typical voluntary organization.

The Motion to Table. It was pointed out in Lesson 9 that in many American organizations the good purposes of the motion to table have been so often perverted that they are difficult to achieve. Good procedure needs a motion by which it can conveniently set aside a piece of business temporarily. When a majority votes to lay a motion on the table in the belief that it is dropping a motion, the vote does not reflect what it should. A chairman seeking to achieve the best uses of parliamentary procedure should, therefore, try to reflect, in his handling of the motion, his conception of its proper purposes. He should, in the first place, not permit it to be used for "sudden death" purposes in place of "objection to consideration"—that is, to silence the proposer and the proponents of a motion before they have had a chance to be heard. So used it is a direct violation of the democratic right of the minority to be heard, because by tabling, a simple majority may throw out a proposal without debate. Democracy dictates that the motion to table should come (1) from one who wishes to set aside the pending motion in order to get at a more urgent matter, (2) by a friend of the motion who believes it might receive more favorable consideration at another time, (3) by an opponent of the motion who believes it might receive less favorable consideration (and possibly no consideration at all), if temporarily set aside, or (4) by one indifferent to the motion but concerned for good procedure who feels that consideration at another time would yield a better decision.

The chairman has no responsibility for seeing to it that matters on the table are taken from it. The initiative must come from a member through the motion to take from the table, which, of course, requires a second, is not debatable, and requires majority support. He needs to remember that the motion comes from the table in the same form as it was put there. If there were amendments pending they are still pending, or if the assembly was considering whether it should be referred to a committee when it was tabled, this becomes the immediately pending question.

The chair needs to remember also that the motion to take from the table has a prior right over any other motion that might have been proposed and has not yet been opened to discussion. Finally, the chair needs to remember that motions left on the table at the end of the session immediately succeeding that at which they were placed there, die there.

Limiting and Closing Debate. The proper use of the motions to limit and close debate, particularly that of closing debate, demands that the chairman not permit them to be misused. Their purpose is to limit the consideration of a motion when further discussion will serve no useful purpose, or will use up time that might better be used otherwise. These motions may very properly be ruled out of order if proposed very early in a heated debate as a gag rule. Not quite so obviously, but similarly, they would not be in order if proposed immediately after the lengthy presentation of an argument for or against the motion to prevent the opposition from replying.

A chairman will accept the motion to close debate either in that wording or the original wording of "moving the previous question," but in the interests of clarity as well as avoiding an awkward statement he will best say, in putting the question, that "it has been moved and seconded to close debate. All those in favor? All those opposed?"

Recess and Adjourn. Because the motions to recess and adjourn are of high privilege, they are a temptation to members to use them for purposes of heckling and also for defeating motions, particularly those that come into consideration toward the end of a long meeting. In other instances a member, anticipating a piece of business that he wants to prevent being considered, will sometimes move to adjourn very quickly after one matter has been finished. When this happens another member may rise, before the vote on adjournment is completed, and announce the important business needing attention. If the members agree that it is important, the assembly will have an opportunity to vote against adjourning. The custom established in many societies by which the chairman terminates the meeting when, in his judgment, it should be ended is a good one and should be encouraged. At the appropriate time he says, "If there is no further business, the meeting is adjourned."

The Special Emergency Procedures. Good procedure in a parliamentary group depends in large measure on the observance of the principle that any particular motion or procedure should be used when and only when it makes procedural sense and is made by a member in good faith. This is particularly true of the special emergency procedures. If they are used for heckling or exhibitionist purposes they are a nuisance. The prime offender can be "point of order." When this becomes the case, the presiding officer should let an offending member know that he considers a particular "point of order" an unwarranted interruption. He may add due notice that similar interruptions of this sort will not be tolerated. In this same connection members making points of order, points of privilege, parliamentary inquiries, and requests for information should be so advised if they have interrupted the proceedings unnecessarily. They have the privilege of immediate decision, action, or answers only if these matters are urgent. When they are not urgent the members should be advised that the answer will be forthcoming, the privilege will be granted, or the point of order will be resolved, when the speaker is finished.

The special procedure that puts the chairman on the spot is the appeal from his decision. By this the member asks the house to reverse a ruling the presiding officer has made, and to a certain extent the prestige of the chairman is in question. He will survive the test best if he realizes that (1) he may be right, (2) the member may be right, or (3) it may be a moot question. Taking this attitude he will wisely first ask the member to state the grounds for his appeal. Following this he can state his own and put the matter to a vote; or if he wishes to be really diplomatic he may say at this point that "the chair is in doubt" and put the decision to the assembly, thereby avoiding a direct vote on whether or not the chair should be sustained or overruled. It should be added here, finally, that the vote on an appeal is put in the form "all those in favor of sustaining the chair raise your hands" and that it takes a majority in the negative to overrule. It is assumed that the chairman will be voting to sustain his ruling. In other words if he votes to break a tie in this case the appeal will be lost.

Taking the Vote. In the preceding paragraph it was pointed out that the chairman may vote to sustain his decision against an appeal. The fact is, of course, that he is entitled to a vote on any question if he wishes to exercise his right, but he does exercise it only when there is some point in doing so. There is point in his doing so only when his vote will make or break a tie vote. If the vote is tied at say 10–10, the motion is, of course, lost since it does not have a majority. If he favors it he may cast his vote with the affirmative and announce that the motion has passed. If the vote is 10 affirmative and 9 negative, he may cast his vote with the negative, making a tie, and causing the motion to be lost. The presiding officer normally does not vote because it is of considerable importance that he maintain always an unbiased and nonpartisan position, avoiding any appearance of taking sides. He does not, however, give up his rights as a member on being elected, and he will therefore exercise his rights whenever he feels it is necessary.

The customary way of taking a vote in most American assemblies is by voice. "All those in favor say 'aye.' Those opposed, 'no'." This has its disadvantages in that the result is difficult to estimate, particularly if there is a loud and enthusiastic minority. It is not the vocal volume but the number of votes that counts. A "show of hands" is better, and there is a growing practice for asking "All those in favor, raise your right hands. Those opposed." If the vote is taken by voice and the result is not clear the chairman should announce that he is in doubt and ask for a "division of the house" taking the vote either by a show of hands or by asking first those in favor, then those opposed, to rise. Any member may call for a division, but the chairman is not required to count the vote unless he is ordered to do so by the motion to that effect duly passed by the assembly.

Most decisions are made by a majority vote, and it is the number voting that counts, irrespective of the number present, unless the constitution specifies that in a particular matter a majority of the total membership or a majority of those present is needed for passage. A two-thirds vote is also computed on the basis of votes cast, unless otherwise specified, and here there is a handy answer to the problem for non-mathematically inclined presiding officers who under the stress of presiding sometimes have difficulty deciding what is two-thirds. In a two-thirds vote if the negative vote doubled equals or exceeds the affirmative, the motion is lost. If the negative vote doubled is less than the affirmative, the motion is carried.

The Fine Art of Presiding.   There is the basic art of presiding in the direction of the procedure. And there is a fine art in good chairmanship that rests more in certain special qualities of the man who performs this task.

What these qualities are might make a lengthy list, but at the top of it we would find those that give us a chairman who is (1) poised, (2) purposeful, and (3) impersonal.

Poise is self-possession, self-assurance, and self-confidence. They arise in us of themselves when we know we have command of a situation, and this is as necessary in a parliamentary group as it is in a company on the battlefield. When there is no confidence in the leadership, the group disintegrates. The presiding officer does not command, but he is in charge and any outward sign that he is not equal to this task of leadership destroys not only his effectiveness but that of the group. The first step in cultivating poise as a chairman is that of earning the right to command the situation by learning the procedure. You cannot preside with self-assurance without the inner conviction that comes from your knowledge of what to do when. The second step is to show this in your behavior. There are such simple and obvious outward manifestations of poise and confidence as stepping resolutely to the rostrum, banging instead of tapping the gavel, speaking loudly, distinctly, and firmly, and ruling quickly with the firm, falling inflections of declarative rather than interrogative sentences. To be a poised presiding officer, then, one needs to deserve it by his inner knowledge of his task, and then to show he deserves it by behaving (acting, if you will) in a way consistent with his knowledge.

A purposeful presiding officer is one who behaves in a way that demonstrates that he will not for an instant lose sight of the main object of all that he and the assembly are trying to do. Purposefulness is a twofold quality. It is evidenced in being both businesslike and practical. To be businesslike means to carry on with a fine sense of both the importance of the job and the importance of getting the job done, without dilly-dallying or nonsense. A chairman achieves this by moving the meeting along without question or delay through the order of business, which he knows, and the agenda, which he has prepared himself to handle. How this can best be done is detailed in Lesson 24. Purposefulness in the second sense, of keeping an eye on the essential aims and objects of the proceedings, results in great measure from taking a practical view of parliamentary procedure. This is the sensible view that the procedure should serve the assembly and the assembly should not become a slave to the rules. In most cases the purposes of the assembly will best be served if the rules are followed, but if following them becomes more important their true purposes are not achieved. A purposeful chairman, then, is one who is practical in his enforcement of the rules and businesslike in the procedure.

To be impersonal should be the third aim of a chairman—impersonal in the sense of unbiased and objective. In describing the nature of his task we might say that it has much in common with that of a referee or umpire. His decisions must be made for and against a crowd that is often partisan and usually divided. Inevitably, in a full term of office, any chairman will rule contrary to the wishes of most of his fellow members, at one time or another. If he shows prejudice, bias, and partiality he will inevitably lose not only all his friends, but his effectiveness to preside as well. On the other hand, a chairman who rules impartially and objectively and remains impersonal will continue to be accepted and respected for the job he is doing.

Last but not least in the qualities of chairmanship is courtesy. Some more than others may be to this manner born, but courtesy is a quality that can be cultivated. Anyone, by trying, can be a little more civil, tactful, thoughtful, gracious, and diplomatic. Everyone should try all of the time, everywhere, of course; but the chairman should try harder because he sets the tone of his meeting, and where a meeting is run as an affair among courteous gentlemen and ladies, half the burden of his task is lifted.

Lesson 23:
The Science of Presiding—Enforcing the Rules

In the preceding lesson on the *art* of presiding we considered how the chairman handles the procedures. In this lesson on the *science* of presiding we will consider the rules the chairman must interpret and enforce in handling these procedures. As a practical problem this is a matter of knowing four things about each motion and procedure

1. Is it in order?
2. Does it need a second?
3. Is it debatable?
4. What vote is required?

There are three ways in which the chairman may solve this problem. He may preside with a chart in front of him and look up the answer each time. He may memorize the answers for the twelve motions and six special procedures—eighty items in all. Or he can learn to *know* the answers from some general principles that can be derived from a study of these rules. Unless the rules are purely arbitrary, there must be reason and logic behind them. There is, as you shall see.

The Rule of Precedence. When a motion is proposed by a member, or a special procedure is initiated, the chairman must know whether it is in order and can be accepted at the time. To answer this question, Robert in his *Rules,* and most writers of rules after him, have provided a list of motions "in their order of precedence"; when any motion in the scale is before the house, any motion higher in the scale can be made, but any one lower in the scale is out of order. This can be helpful if you keep the list before you as you preside, but only partially helpful, because the chart is riddled with exceptions. There are times when motions lower in the scale may be applied to motions above, and there are

times when motions farther up the line are not in order when
one lower is pending.

There is a practical rule for the precedence of motions, which
can be logically derived and can be applied in any situation:

ANY MOTION OR PROCEDURE IS IN ORDER IF IT MAKES PROCE-
DURAL SENSE AND IS MADE IN GOOD FAITH.

Procedural sense means suited to the natural procedural progression for the transaction of business as it is pictured in Lesson
4. This is the progression from proposal or main motion through
its consideration with the possible application of the five subsidiary motions, the limitation of debate, a vote, and the possibility
of a reversal of the decision by reconsideration or repeal. When
a chairman has before his assembly one main motion that has not
yet been disposed of, it is obvious procedural sense that another
main motion is out of order. On the other hand, when a main
motion or proposal is before the house, such motions as to postpone indefinitely, amend, refer, postpone, and table do fit the
pattern. They do make procedural sense and are therefore in
order. It is obvious, too, that when debate is in progress and has
been for some time, it makes procedural sense to move to limit or
close it. After a motion has been passed, it makes procedural
sense to propose to reconsider or repeal it. This resolves the basic
problem of precedence for ten of the twelve motions. The remaining two, the motions to recess and adjourn, solve their own problems by classification. They are by definition "privileged motions"
that can be made at any time.

By itself, the rule that to be accepted a motion must make
procedural sense is enough to guide the chairman in the matter
of precedence in most situations. It is helpful, however to add
the second part of the rule—that "the motion must be made in
good faith." A motion is made in good faith when it is made for
the good purposes for which it is designed to be used. When it is
made for some ulterior purpose, or with some devious intent, it is
not. When a member moves, for example, to lay a motion on the
table very shortly after a motion has been proposed, not because
the assembly has heard enough, but rather, because he is afraid
of their hearing more from the minority, the motion is not made

in good faith. In such cases and all similar ones, the chairman will properly rule these motions out of order whether they fit the narrow test of procedural sense or not.

This rule places a great deal of responsibility on the judgment of the chair, but it is a fair assumption that he is the person in the assembly most competent to judge, from the standpoint of both knowledge and objectivity. It may also be suggested that such judgment gives the chair autocratic powers not suited to a democratic society. This is not true. The chair always decides with the concurrence of the assembly because at any time any member may appeal from the decision of the chair and the chair may be overruled by the majority.

For the less experienced and less confident chairman who, in a particularly difficult situation, may not wish to take on the responsibility of ruling a motion out of order, there is still the very proper procedure of putting the decision to the assembly. He need only proceed as follows:

Chairman: The chair is in doubt as to whether this motion is in order and should be accepted at this time. All those who would accept it, raise your right hands. Those opposed. The vote is affirmative and the motion is accepted as in order.

There still remains what is really a minor problem in the precedence of motions, in spite of the fact that it often gets attention out of all proper proportion in books of the *rules*. This is the problem of what might be called the internal or relative precedence of the five subsidiary motions:
1. Table.
2. Postpone definitely.
3. Refer to a committee.
4. Amend.
5. Postpone indefinitely.
Because General Robert found that it was the practice of the parliamentary bodies he studied to observe an order of precedence among these five in the order we have listed them, he handed this down to us, and it has been reprinted in parliamentary charts ever since. It means that when any motion lower among these five is being considered, any one higher can be

proposed and must be considered first. Or if any one higher is
being considered, one lower cannot be proposed. By way of
illustration, a chairman following this rule would accept a
motion to refer a proposal to a committee in the course of the
discussion on whether or not the assembly should postpone it
indefinitely; or, in the same situation, he might accept the motion
to amend, or to postpone definitely, or to table. He would not,
however, accept the motion to refer to a committee, or either of
the other two lower in the scale while the assembly was considering whether or not to postpone definitely.

The problem with the charts is that there are exceptions. It is
an error, for example, to conclude that because the motion to
amend is lower than the motion to postpone definitely, an amendment is out of order when postponing definitely is under consideration, as the charts imply. The fact is that the motion to
postpone definitely may be amended. If it is proposed to postpone a motion to three o'clock, a member may move to modify
the time. The same is true for the motion to refer to a committee.
This may also be modified as the assembly chooses, particularly
in the number of its members or how they are to be selected.
Any motion that has details in it that permit choice, such as the
two already mentioned and the motion to recess (where five
minutes or ten minutes or more or less may be chosen), may be
amended. It makes procedural sense to amend them, and for this
reason we say again that the best guide line for the chairman in
the matter of precedence is that a motion is in order and should
be accepted when it makes procedural sense and is made in good
faith.

In this discussion of the precedence of motions we have not
adverted to the special emergency procedures. There is no precedence among them. They are called *incidental motions* because
they arise incidentally out of the course of business, and when
they are initiated they are disposed of immediately (as parenthetical incidents) and nothing is permitted to intervene. In one sense
they are, as a group, all of the highest precedence in that they
are in order whenever a situation arises that in the judgment of
a member calls for them. Practically, this means that whenever
a member rises to a point of order or privilege, or appeals, or

objects, or requests information, the chairman has no choice but to hear the member out except where the procedure is not initiated in good faith. As we have pointed out before, repeated points of order raised to heckle the speaker or the chairman or to disrupt the assembly are not in order and should be so ruled.

There remains a final problem, related to the problem of the precedence of motions, usually referred to in books of the rules as the "renewability" in motions. It is in practice the question of how soon a motion or procedure, once disposed of, can be proposed a second time. For example, if a motion to table is proposed and defeated, and later in the discussion, on the same main motion, some member proposes it again, is it in order? The answer is that if in the intervening time, it is reasonable to assume that additional members might have changed their minds and would now favor tabling the motion, then it is in order. The same reasoning would apply to other subsidiary motions, such as postponing definitely or referring to a committee, and to the motions to close and limit debate. The rule in parliamentary practice is that no assembly should be asked the same question twice, with the distinction that in new situations, or at a later time, a question asked in the same words is in reality a new question. A motion to close debate, previously defeated, may well become a new question an hour later, and therefore the proposal of it may make procedural sense a second time. It is for the chairman to judge. The assembly may overrule him by appeal if it disagrees, so here again the basic rule that a motion must make procedural sense and be made in good faith is the answer to the question of the renewability of motions.

Is a Second Required?   After accepting a motion the chairman must know whether or not it needs a second. The rule can be stated simply:

ALL MOTIONS REQUIRE A SECOND. THE SPECIAL PROCEDURES (EXCEPT APPEAL) DO NOT.

The simplicity of this rule may come as a revelation to many students of parliamentary procedure (and something of a shock to seasoned parliamentarians) but is a legitimate and completely operative rule, in the context of the classifications of motions and procedures made throughout this book. There are the twelve motions, all properly so called because when proposed, the member says, "I move that . . ." The special procedures are not initiated as a motion with "I move that" but rather as "points," "appeals," "objections," and so on. So the chairman need only remember that if the member said "I move that" he is "making a motion" and needs a second.

The special emergency procedures (except appeal) do not need a second. A member rising for a point of order or privilege, to raise a question or to object to consideration needs no second. This is reasonable because each of these is an individual matter in which he is on his own. The appeal from the decision of the chair is made an exception to prevent one obstreperous member on his own from abusing this procedure. It is the only special procedure on which remarks are permitted, and here is where the abuse could arise.

With respect to the requirement of the second, the chairman should remember its purpose—to prevent the assembly from being forced to consider a proposal from a man who does not recruit anyone in its immediate support. One could argue the validity of this motion, particularly its consistency to true democracy, because we all know that history is filled with examples in which one man had to wage quite a good fight before he recruited any followers. We could argue also that in a democracy we ought to give one man, with God on his side, a chance to become a majority. The requirement of a second is, however, a good and useful one in parliamentary practice. Parliamentarians, and sometimes even beginning student practitioners of the procedure, however, often make too much of the second. They have been known to ask whether or not a motion that was never seconded is legally passed. Both common sense and good democracy should make it obvious that whether or not there was a second is of little consequence if the motion was discussed, debated, and passed by a substantial majority. From this standpoint a chairman should remember that if a motion is presented with evidence of the support of one or more additional members, no second should be called for. This is true in a motion made by the chairman of a committee to adopt its recommendations, because in this case we would have support from other members of the committee. This would be true also in the case where a member moved that the proposer of a motion should be permitted to accept an amendment that he has offered to accept. This is also true in a different way in many legislative bodies such as houses of delegates in national conventions. Here each delegate is a representative of many members and his motions may be assumed to have the support of those he represents, so no second should be required.

To sum it up, then, the chairman may safely be guided by the rule that all motions require a second if they are really motions and he hears the member introduce it with "I move that . . . " The special procedures do not, except the appeal from the decision of the chair.

Is It Debatable? After a motion has been made and seconded, before the chairman can say, "Is there any discussion?" he needs to know whether the motion is debatable, because if it is not he must proceed at once to a vote. Here again there is a relatively simple rule that can furnish the answer, and it will be easily remembered if the history and the logic from which it comes are understood. It is probably true that in the beginning every motion, when it was first used, was presented with some argument, or at least some explanation for it by the proposer, followed by some rebuttal and even extended debate. It was found however, that to permit the proposer of a procedural motion, such as the motion to table, to present an argument for laying it on the table and then to permit a reply from someone opposed inevitably led into a full-scale debate on the original proposal. This defeated the purpose of tabling, which was, of course, to set aside the discussion to another time. The same is true to a large extent for all the procedural motions. If we begin to debate whether or not to adjourn or close debate or some similar procedure, we inevitably get involved in a discussion of the merits of the pending main motion, thereby defeating the purpose of the procedural motion. We not only defeat its basic purpose, but we also lose the incidental value of many such motions, in that they are intended to be a quick and effective way to decide a procedural matter. These questions are different from substantive questions that involve fundamental matters in transacting the business of an assembly. It is the purpose of discussion and debate to enable an assembly to become informed so that it can make an intelligent decision related to a proposition it has before it. How it shall proceed in arriving at that decision is not a question on which extensive discussion or unlimited debate is likely to be either necessary or profitable.

On the basis of the above reasoning, all motions that are substantive, that actually transact business and dispose of it finally, permit of unlimited debate. These are the main motion, the motion to amend, postpone indefinitely, and the two that undo business, reconsider and repeal. A main motion is in essence substantive. An amendment alters the substance of a main motion. The motion to repeal is as substantive as the main motion in that it reverses the original action. The motion to postpone indefinitely drops finally a proposal (which is substantive) and the motion to reconsider leads to its undoing. The motions to postpone indefinitely and to reconsider belong in the unlimited-debate category also because in practice they cannot be logically debated without injecting the merits of the main motion to which they refer into the argument. Their discussion inevitably becomes substantive.

The procedural motions are not open to unlimited debate. The motions to table, to close debate, and to adjourn are strictly undebatable and are voted immediately after being seconded and stated by the chair. The same would probably be true for the four remaining procedural motions—to postpone definitely, refer, limit debate, and recess—except for the fact that each of them permits the proposer to qualify them to his own individual taste in some way, and this should be subject to modification by the assembly. When one moves to postpone definitely he sets a time of his choice, when he moves to limit debate he says by how much, and when he moves to recess he says for how long. When a member moves to refer to a committee there is a choice of who is to be on it, what it is to do, and when it is to report. This necessarily opens these motions for special consideration and possible amendment. To enable the assembly to make these choices, amendments are permitted. These motions may be qualified, and the qualifications need to be discussed if they are to be democratically selected. For this reason four motions are usually listed in the charts as permitting limited debate—that is, debate limited to the procedural question.

The special emergency procedures are undebatable. An impression that there is an exception to this may be gained from some charts and texts because the chairman may permit a member who appeals from the decision to state the grounds for his appeal. To this the chairman may reply, stating his position; but this does not in any true sense make it debatable. The rules specify that in such a case neither this member nor any other should be permitted to speak a second time in this situation—that is, debate is not permitted.

To sum it up, then, the problems of debatability are solved for the chairman if he will apply the following rule:

MOTIONS RESULTING IN SUBSTANTIVE DECISIONS ARE DEBATABLE. THE UNQUALIFIED PROCEDURAL MOTIONS AND SPECIAL PROCEDURES ARE UNDEBATABLE, QUALIFIED OR QUALIFIABLE MOTIONS PERMIT LIMITED DEBATE.

It will be helpful to the chairman to keep always in mind this rule that the motions that do business (main motions) and undo business (reconsider and repeal), and the motion to amend (change the substance of a motion) and to postpone indefinitely (drop a motion) are the debatable ones. All other motions are concerned with how to proceed rather than a substantive decision. If these are originally complete in themselves, as are the motions to adjourn, close debate, and table, they are undebatable. If they are originally incomplete, as are recess, limit debate, refer to a committee, and postpone definitely, and need to be filled out by the member, they permit of limited debate. This last may be said in another way by pointing out that the procedural motions that are *amendable* permit of limited debate.

What Vote Is Required?   The last question confronting the presiding officer in the handling of a motion is the vote required —majority or two thirds? Here the rule can be stated simply, and a brief explanation will suffice to provide the chairman the logical background to remember it:

ALL DECISIONS ARE MADE BY A MAJORITY VOTE EXCEPT THOSE
TO UPSET BASIC PRINCIPLES OR DECISIONS PREVIOUSLY MADE.

Majority rule is a principle of democracy and parliamentary procedure operates under this principle. It is only when this principle comes into conflict with other principles that an exception must be made. There is, first of all, the principle of full and free debate with which the motions to close debate and the procedure of objecting to consideration come in conflict. There is also the principle of government under law in democracy—what is agreed to, passed, and established shall stand and be abided by—and with this the motion to repeal, upsetting a decision previously made, comes into conflict. For these reasons the motions to close and limit debate, and to repeal, and the procedure of objecting to consideration require a two-thirds vote. All others take a simple majority.

Lesson 24:
Running a Meeting—The Order of Business

A potential chairman who has profited from Lesson 22 on the art of presiding knows the nature and purpose of the task he faces and is likely to take the proper attitude toward it. If he has learned the rules as they are set down in Lesson 23 he knows the answers to the questions of precedence, seconding, debatability and the vote. This brings him to the point where he is ready to step up before the assembly, take the gavel, and call the meeting to order. In this lesson we turn to the problem of running a meeting.

The chairman "runs" a meeting as a traffic officer "runs things" on a busy corner. He keep things moving. If he does not, either everything stops, goes very badly, or perhaps ends in a chaotic muddle. Good meetings depend on good presiding officers. Good meetings that get things done efficiently, and with a minimum loss of time, depend first upon having a good man in the chair.

Good meetings do not begin with the first rap of the gavel that calls them to order. For the chairman who is willing to plan, there are things that can be planned. Most meetings have fixed matters for their agenda, and some thought can be given to how best these will be handled. If there is an election to be held, the president will make sure he knows what the constitution or by-laws provide about the method of the nominations and elections, and he makes sure that ballots will be available if they are needed. If there are certain important items that must be disposed of, he makes sure that his meeting does not get bogged down in inconsequential details, to the detriment of the proper consideration of what is important. Although it is not the prerogative of the chairman to tell his assembly what can be considered at a particular meeting, a methodical and efficient chairman with a bit of diplomacy can usually manage to suggest the items that in his judgment deserve prior consideration. If this unofficial agenda makes sense, it will usually be accepted.

Beyond mere business matters—if there are special guests to be present, a speaker to be heard, materials to be distributed, facts, figures, slides, or films to be presented, or even coffee and donuts to be served—the capable presiding officer double checks with those responsible to see that what is needed will be available when it is needed.

Calling the Meeting to Order. When the members have assembled, or perhaps better, at the time the meeting is set to begin, the presiding officer calls it to order. We say preferably at the time set because the too-well-established custom in many American clubs and societies of getting underway fifteen minutes or a half hour late is unfair to those who come on time and is a reflection on the president. Starting a little late is an outgrowth of what is at first a little dilly-dallying that eventually develops into a "public nuisance."

The meeting is called to order by pounding the gavel on the table. The presiding officer should have a gavel because it makes presiding easier. When the going gets rough, exasperation and lack of composure is likely to be shown by a voice pleading for order. Pounding on the table is better. There is a technique to it, too. Experienced presiding officers have found that giving two nicely spaced and deliberate raps on the table, followed by a pause for complete attention during which they look intently to any points where it does not seem to be forthcoming, is most effective. They wait for complete attention, and only when all is quiet they say, "Will the meeting please come to order?"

Many meetings begin with a prayer, and this practice has some extratheological reasons to recommend it. As old, experienced teachers long ago learned in the classroom, there was nothing like a prayer after recess to simmer things down to quiet, serious business. To the contemporary view that there may be something offensive in prayer in a democratic group, we can reply that our Founding Fathers invariably began their meetings this way, as do such reasonably democratic bodies as the House and Senate of the United States.

The Order of Business.   When the chairman has his house in order, his next words are usually to the secretary, requesting the reading of the minutes of the last meeting. This is the beginning of the conventional "order of business," usually prescribed by the constitution or bylaws, which in turn are usually copied from *Robert's Rules of Order.* If specified, normally the order will be as *Robert's Rules* directs—that is, as follows:

1. Reading of the minutes.
2. Reports of standing committees.
3. Reports of special committees.
4. Unfinished business.
5. New business.

This order is mandatory. If any member wishes to take up a matter out of this order, he must move to suspend the rules and he will need a second and a two-thirds vote to have it done.

The Reading of the Minutes.   The *minutes* is the secretary's account of what happened at the preceding meeting. It is for all a review of what has gone before and an indication of the state of things. For those who were absent at the previous meeting it is a report of what happened. It gives each member a chance to point out an omission, to make revisions and corrections, and it gives the organization a chance to place its final stamp of approval on what becomes the official record of the transactions of the group. It is with these purposes in mind, after the opening prayer or when the meeting comes to order, that the presiding officer says:

Chairman: Will the secretary please read the minutes of our last meeting?

Right here at the outset, as the secretary begins to intone what for many may be "old hat," is the place where good order so often begins to deteriorate, where attention lags, and where whispered conversations begin, so this may be the place where the presiding officer has a good opportunity to demonstrate that he intends to maintain good order. The secretary has a duty to make himself heard, and the members have a duty to listen. At the first sign that this is not happening, one good rap on the table, again with a pause for silence, followed by, "Will the meeting please come to order?" may be needed. Where this approach is too blunt, more diplomatic presiding officers sometimes rap gently on the table to stop the secretary and make some such observation as, "Some of the members are having difficulty hearing. Can the secretary be heard in the rear of the room?" When the secretary has finished, the proper line is as follows:

Chairman: Are there any additions or corrections to the minutes? (*and after a pause*) If not, the minutes stand approved as read.

The practice of waiting for a motion to accept the minutes and then asking for one if it is not forthcoming is pointless. If there are no additions or corrections to the minutes, they are assumed to be satisfactory to everyone and therefore approved.

If a member has an addition or a correction it is usually accepted by the chairman and approved by general consent by his saying, "If there is no objection the secretary will make the correction." If a member objects to the correction, then it is up to the assembly to decide whether or not it should be made. The quickest and best way for settling the matter is for the chairman to say:

> *Chairman:* Since objection has been raised to the correction, the house will decide. All those in favor of the correction, raise your right hand. Those opposed. There being a majority in the affirmative the secretary will make the correction. (*or if the vote is negative,* The minutes will stand as read.)

The above procedure will serve in most instances where the correction is a matter based primarily on minor differences of opinion between two members. If the matter is of some consequence and of some concern and interest to a large majority of the members, then the chairman should proceed formally with a motion, second, and discussion of the change. The chairman will best ask the proposer of the revision if he would like to make a formal motion indicating precisely how he would amend the minutes.

After a correction or revision the chairman should not forget to provide further opportunity for corrections, and when there are no more his lines are, "The minutes stand approved as corrected."

Treasurer's Report. Organizations (with expenses, money, and a balance) will usually hear of their finances following the minutes. This report will vary with the magnitude of the finances involved. The treasurer may report income, item by item, and expenses in the same detail. In other instances he will report the income and list the bills to be paid, and the membership will approve their payment. Here again, as in the case of the minutes, there is no need to extract a formal motion to pay the bills from the floor. The chairman can expedite the matter by a vote of general consent as follows:

> *Chairman:* If there is no objection, these bills are ordered paid.

There is an important distinction between hearing the report of the treasurer and approving it. If it is to be approved, then it should be listened to as an audit of his account and it should be possible from the listening to judge it as such. Normally this is not the case. Most organizations have auditors or accountants who attest to the accuracy of the bookkeeping from time to time, and normally, therefore, a treasurer's report is heard for information only. In this case all that is necessary to complete the procedure is for the chairman to say:

Chairman: You have heard the treasurer's report. Are there any questions? . . . The report is accepted.

Reports of Standing Committees. A committee is a group of people given a specific job to do; a standing committee is set up by the constitution or by-laws for a regular term, usually the same as the other officers, and is given the job of concerning itself with a certain category or part of the business of the organization. There may be a committee on membership or finance. There may be a committee charged with getting speakers, developing programs, or arranging entertainment and social events. Reports from these committees are heard at this point to let the members know what they are up to, whether or not they have any plans afoot, any problems to report, or any projects to propose. At this point their reports are heard for information only. In accepting each report the assembly gives its approval to what is being done. If the committee makes a proposal on a relatively minor, routine matter, the chair will give it the "go ahead" on the assumption that the assembly is giving general assent. But if the committee has a major project or plan it wishes to propose, then this is new business and should be brought up later in the meeting in the form of a motion.

The chairman introduces the standing committee reports by calling for them in order with the following:

Chairman: Is the membership committee ready to report, Mr. Jones?

Jones is presumably the chairman of the committee, and he is responsible for the report, and is by this statement of the chair given the floor to report for the committee. When he has finished, the chairman concludes the matter by the following:

Chairman: Are there any questions or suggestions for the committee? . . . If there is no objection the committee will go ahead as it proposes, and its report is accepted.

Special Committees. A special committee is given a certain job to do, and it is given a day to report. When that day comes, the report is heard at this point in the order of business. The chairman calls for such reports as in the case of standing committees by asking whether the chairman of the committee on so-and-so is ready to report. Because a special committee very often has a specific recommendation to make, and usually has a piece of business that originated at a previous meeting, this proposal may properly be classified as unfinished business.

If, for example, at a previous meeting, it had been proposed that the organization cooperate in the efforts of local groups to get out the vote on Election Day, and if this had been referred to a special committee to explore ways and means to do this, the committee may now report its conclusion that the club should rent five automobiles to transport voters to the polls. In this case the committee chairman should be asked to put this recommendation in the form of a motion. If he does so, it is taken up at once.

In the case just described the special committee was given the job of studying the proposal and suggesting what should be done. In other cases special committees are given a job to do, such as finding a new meeting place, getting a speaker for the annual banquet, selecting a convention city, or collecting money for the Boy Scouts. In this case, the committee reports for information only, and the report is handled as in the case of the standing committee.

It is important for the sake of courtesy for the chairman to thank a special committee that has rendered its report, but it is more important to indicate that the committee is now dissolved and discharged, because such is the case. This is important in larger organizations because temporary committees, like temporary government bureaus, have a tendency to become permanent.

Postponed and Unfinished Business. Many organizations call unfinished business "old" business. It is better to think of this as the proper place for matters postponed to this meeting, and items unfinished at the previous one. The term *old* is a popular one, but it is not a good one, because it suggests that this is the place to bring up the tired, old, perennial problems on which the organization has generally gotten nowhere. Postponed business should come first, and here the presiding officer should continue to exercise the leadership of a traffic policeman, indicating what should move. Postponed business means matters set aside by the motion to postpone definitely to this particular meeting. If there are many such matters the chairman may exercise his judgment on what should come first, or if the members object then the rule is that they should be taken up in the order in which they were postponed. We go to this item like this:

Chairman: Under the heading of postponed business the first item is the matter of having some new copies of our Constitution made. The motion was that the secretary be instructed to have 500 copies of our Constitution reprinted. Is there any discussion?

Unfinished business includes both items that were interrupted by the adjournment of the previous meeting and items that were laid on the table—but only if a member moves to take them up. Here, instead of indicating what will be taken up, the chair merely asks

Chairman: Are there any items of unfinished business that any member would like to bring before this meeting?

This distinction is important because matters laid on the table should stay there until a member desires that they be taken from it. When an assembly adjourns with business pending, it does so without any commitment to take up the pending matter again, and with a full realization that the next meeting is a new and different one.

New Business. It is under the heading of new business that organizations really get down to business, and unless an agenda is prescribed for this part of the meeting by the constitution, or has been set by a committee on agenda, and adopted, this is a free-wheeling operation in which the initiative passes from the presiding officer to the members. He may wisely exercise some guidance where he feels it would be helpful, as in the situation that might prompt the following opening observation:

Chairman: We proceed now to new business. I would like to invite the attention of the members to the fact that certain urgent matters must be settled at this meeting, including the selection of our delegates to the national convention and the adoption of the resolutions they are to take to the convention. Tonight we must decide whether we will participate again in the Fourth of July observance, and we must also decide whether we are going to renew our contract for this building. If possible also we should decide tonight what we are going to do about the honorary memberships, and whether or not the spring picnic should be held. New business is now in order. What is the first matter to come before the meeting?

For the Good of the Order.   There is a nice old tradition that has added a final item in the order of business before adjournment called *for the good of the order.* This probably developed in fraternal and benevolent organizations and from them has spread to unions, fraternities, sororities, and all sorts of other American clubs and societies. It probably came to be in meetings at which the chairman was not pushed for time and members were enjoying themselves and feeling no particular desire to rush home. After the question from the chair, "Is there any further business to come before the house?" there was none and there was no motion to adjourn. Instead of sending them home with the usual "If there is no further business, the meeting is adjourned," he said, "Is there anything anyone would like to bring up for the good of our society?" So put it was an invitation to all of the members not to get something off their chests, but rather to say something that was on their minds. Today, where the practice persists, it still exists in this spirit, and it provides a place with a kind of fraternal informality. Almost anything can be brought up without the usual formalities of parliamentary procedure.

For the good of the order as a category of *business* is not mentioned in and therefore has no standing under a strict interpretation of *Robert's Rules,* and many parliamentarians view it with a jaundiced eye. They argue that if a matter is a proper item of business for a group, there is a place for it.

This is a logical position, but it is also a stuffy one. When a group has time and is in the mood, it can well use a free-wheeling session devoted to longer term suggestions, off-the-cuff observations, and pertinent reminders for the general good. At the same time, it is good to provide a time for such smaller courtesies, generous gestures, and human and fraternal observations as reminding the members to support the charity drive, that brother Smith is still in the hospital, or that Mrs. Townsend is doing a first-class job with the Cub Scouts and should be commended.

Adjourning the Meeting. Normally a meeting is adjourned when it has completed its business, and this has happened when the chair gets no response to his question on whether there is any further business to come before the meeting. If there is not, he will best adjourn the meeting by general consent saying, "If there is no further business the meeting is adjourned."

More properly it might be argued that he say, "If there is no further business, a motion to adjourn is in order," or "Will someone please move to adjourn?" but there is no point in this time-consuming formality in the typical, voluntary organization.

PART III

Broadening
your Knowledge

SKILL in parliamentary procedure will have its foundation built in the knowledge that can be gleaned from the preceding pages and its superstructure erected in the practice suggested in the pages that follow.

In Lesson 25 which follows there is set forth the procedure by which an organization is formed. This will be useful information to anyone involved in the beginning, or instrumental in the founding, of any association society or club. It is at the same time an exercise of particular utility with worthwhile objectives for a class in parliamentary procedure. It is a step by step procedure, and each of the steps is a practical problem in the solution of which there is something worthwhile to be learned.

The following Lesson 26 complements the preceding one, and will normally be carried out in conjunction with it.

The exercise of writing a constitution has much to recommend it for any student. It is a salutary experience for anyone to be forced to set down in the formal language of articles and sections words that will convey the same precise meaning both today and to subsequent readers and this, of course, is a basic requirement of a constitution.

Lesson 27 outlines 12 class exercises in an order of progressive difficulty derived by the author in many years of class experience. Each is aimed to cultivate skill in a particular aspect of the procedure, and together their objectives are calculated to add up to a full and well-rounded knowledge of parliamentary procedure.

There is added, finally, a limited but very carefully selected bibliography. It includes the authoritative and basic references on the Rules, several other textbooks, some books of unique historic interest, some of international interest, and finally one on the legal aspects of parliamentary procedure.

Lesson 25:
Forming an Organization

With the number of organizations existing in this country, it is amazing how few people know how, properly, to go about forming one. At the rate new organizations come into existence, how to organize one is a piece of knowledge almost anyone is likely to find worth knowing sometime. For these reasons we set forth below a step-by-step procedure that not only is simple and efficient but also satisfies all of the requirements of good democracy and good parliamentary practice. It takes you from the initial assembly of the prospective members to the end of the second meeting, when the organization is in business and ready to function.

First Meeting.

Step 1—Assembling the Prospective Members. In the most convenient and effective way those people who may be interested or prospective members should be brought together. This may be by word of mouth, notices on bulletin boards, or by mail invitation.

Step 2—Establishing Order. When the prospective members have gathered, one person (anyone) rises and, either from his place, or stepping before the group to get attention says:

Will the assembly please come to order? (*and after it does*) I move that we agree to operate temporarily according to accepted parliamentary practice. Is there a second? All in favor? Opposed? The motion is carried. This meeting will proceed according to standard parliamentary procedure.

Step 3—Choosing Temporary Officers. Having agreed to follow standard procedure, the assembly needs a presiding officer and a secretary who may be selected as follows if the same member or any other continues:

Any Member: Would someone like to suggest a temporary chairman?
Another Member: I move that Mr. Smith act as temporary chairman.
First Member (after second): It has been moved and seconded that Mr. Smith act as temporary chairman. All those in favor, say 'aye.' Those opposed, 'no.' The motion is carried. Will Mr. Smith please take the chair?
Temporary Chairman (after assuming chair): Is there a suggestion for a temporary secretary?
Member: I move that Miss Jones act as temporary secretary.
Chairman (after second): The motion is that Miss Jones act as temporary secretary. All those in favor. All those opposed. The motion is carried. Will Miss Jones please join me up here in the capacity of secretary?

Step 4—Passing the Organizing Proposal. With the meeting in order, a presiding officer in charge, and the secretary prepared to record the proceedings, the meeting is ready for the business for which it was called. This is initiated best as follows:

Chairman: What is the business to come before this meeting?
Member: I move that we form a permanent organization for the purposes of . . . (*stating general purposes of organization*).
Chairman (after second): It has been moved and seconded that we form a permanent organization . . . Is there any discussion?

This is the place for the proposer of the motion and the prime movers in this project to have their say on what they have in mind, a place where the purposes of the proposed organization can be discussed and clarified and the basic decision made to form the organization. It is assumed that this motion will be passed. If it is not the meeting will obviously adjourn and the organization will not be formed.

Step 5—Appointing a Constitutional Committee. If the organizing motion is passed, the next step is to get a constitution drawn up and to adopt it. The chairman will remind the assembly of this if it is necessary. The procedure is the following:

Member: I move that the chairman appoint a committee of three to draft a proposed constitution for this organization, and to report at the next meeting.

Chairman (after second): It has been moved and seconded that the chairman appoint a constitutional committee. If there is no discussion and no objection the chairman appoints Hammond, Carroll, and Laine to constitute a committee to draft a proposed constitution to be brought in for adoption at our next meeting.

Step 6—Adjourn to Meet Again. The business for this meeting is now concluded. It remains only to fix the time to meet again and to adjourn.

Second Meeting.

Step 1—Call to Order. At the appointed time the temporary chairman calls the meeting to order and the assembly hears the minutes of the first meeting.

Step 2—Adoption of the Constitution. After the minutes have been approved, the chairman calls for the report of the constitution committee, which is presented by the committee chairman, with the following:

Chairman: The main motion before the house will be on the adoption of the constitution to be read by the chairman of the committee. Will the chairman please read the first article?

The committee chairman will then read Article 1, at the conclusion of which the presiding chairman will ask if there is any discussion or any proposed amendment to the article. If there are motions to amend the article, these are treated in the usual way as explained in Lesson 6.

The constitution is read, article by article, with opportunities for discussion and amendment provided after the reading of each one. After the last article has been so treated, the chairman asks if there are any amendments to the preamble or to the constitution as a whole. When this has been disposed of, the vote on the original motion to adopt the constitution is taken and if it is passed by a majority vote, the constitution goes into effect immediately.

Step 3—Election of Officers. After the constitution is adopted, the new organization begins to operate immediately, proceeding at once to its first order of business, the election of officers as specified in the constitution. After they are elected, they are installed and the organization is in business.

Lesson 26:
Drafting a Constitution

The constitution of an organization expresses the reasons for its existence, brings it into being, and gives it continued existence. It is a contract men make with one another when it is adopted—an agreement each new member promises to live by and a compact the officers solemnly swear or tacitly agree to support when they take office.

There is an art (of rhetoric) to writing a constitution and a science (political science) in framing its articles, particularly because these articles must set up the mechanics by which the society will be governed. The problem in writing a constitution is to say clearly and succinctly what should be said so that it may stand, preferably for all time.

Most constitutions are too long. They are so because they are written by people who in their zeal to do a thorough job include all sorts of unnecessary provisions that are covered by accepted parliamentary practice, and therefore are already specified in the rules the organization agrees to live by.

The constitution for a new organization should be conceived as a minimum instrument specifying only what is necessary with the view that it will be regularly reviewed, revised, and added to as the experience of the group indicates and makes necessary.

Essentially a constitution should state: (1) the purpose, (2) the name, (3) the specifications for membership, (4) the officers, (5) the meetings, (6) the parliamentary authority, and (7) the method of amendment. What the typical beginning organization needs beyond this will usually either be specified in *Robert's Rules* or can be learned only through operational experience.

The best solution of the problem for anyone charged with preparing the draft of the constitution is to find a good model in another organization of a similar kind, and use it as a guide. We furnish below such a model, developed in its original form by a hard-working constitutional committee and hammered into shape in a subsequent organizational meeting.

Preamble

For purposes deemed wise and good, hereinafter set forth, an organization is hereby established submitting itself to be governed by, and dedicating itself to uphold the following constitution.

Article One—Purpose

It shall be the purpose of this organization to provide an opportunity for its members to enlarge their knowledge of *Robert's Rules* and develop their skills in parliamentary procedure in regular meetings and through special programs as specified in Article five in this constitution.

Article Two—Name

The name of this organization shall be the Jefferson Society.

Article Three—Membership

Section One. Active members in this organization shall consist of those whose names have been inscribed as charter members to this constitution and those additional persons who may be elected to membership.

Section Two. Active membership in this organization shall be open to any undergraduate students in this University who have completed satisfactorily one semester of college work and who have been elected to membership as provided in Section Three of this article.

Section Three. Members shall be elected at the first meeting of each month by majority vote by secret ballot on the recommendation of three members submitted in writing to the secretary at a previous meeting.

Section Four. Honorary membership may be conferred on any member of the faculty or staff of this University by a majority vote of the members on the recommendation of the Executive Committee.

Article Four—Officers

Section One. The officers of this organization shall consist of a president, vice-president, secretary, two directors, and a speaker of the house. Their duties shall be those normally associated with those offices and as prescribed in traditional parliamentary practice.

Section Two. The president, vice-president, secretary, and directors shall be elected for a term of six months by nominations from the floor and secret ballot.

Section Three. The speaker of the house shall be appointed at each regular meeting by the president immediately following the reading of the minutes to preside from that time until the adjournment of the meeting.

Section Four. The president, vice-president, secretary, and directors shall constitute an executive committee of this society to plan meetings and programs and to assume such other duties as may be assigned by the membership from time to time.

Article Five—Meetings

Section One. Regular meetings of this society shall be held each Wednesday at 3:00 p.m. in those weeks when the University is in session.

Section Two. Special meetings may be called by the president and must be called by him at the written request of one third of the members.

Section Three. A quorum for any meeting shall consist of a majority of the active membership.

Article Six—Rules of Procedure

Accepted American parliamentary practice as set forth in *Robert's Rules* shall govern the conduct of the affairs of this society and the procedure of its meetings.

Article Seven—Amendments

This constitution may be amended at any regular meeting by a two-thirds vote, provided due notice has been given at the preceding regular meeting.

Lesson 27:
Class Exercises

Listed below are a dozen class exercises, one for each of the weeks that might be available in the typical college course.

These are recommended for extensive use, along with others

the teacher and students may devise. Parliamentary procedure is best learned through practice. What students will learn about procedure in a formal course will be inversely proportional to how much the teacher talks about it, and directly proportional to how much the students practice.

Exercise 1—Framing Motions.   Knowledge and skill for framing good motions, petitions, recommendations, and resolutions are prerequisite for effective participation in meetings. Each member of the class will write out two of each for class and teacher criticism on the basis of the criteria set forth in Lesson 3.

Exercise 2—The Core Procedure.   The core procedure should be habitual and second nature for presiding officers and members. This will come about through practice and drill, with members of the class alternating in the chair, each calling for new business, accepting a motion, and taking it through the series of steps set forth in Lesson 2 (omitting discussion) to the announcement of the decision.

Exercise 3—Proposal Speeches.   Good practice in parliamentary procedure and excellent training in parliamentary speaking will be provided in the presentation of three-to-five minute proposal speeches following the proposal of main motions by each member of the class. These preferably will deal with some problem suited to treatment as a recommendation, petition, or resolution as explained in Lesson 3. In one of these forms they may deal with campus, local, state, or national problems of concern to the proposer and interest to the class, to the end that they will create a realistic speaking situation.

Exercise 4—Parliamentary Debate.   Exercise 3 can next be broadened either all the way to unlimited debate, or to limited debate only—permitting two or three members to respond to the proposal, followed by a one-minute closing speech by the proposer. This will provide him training in the skills of impromptu rebuttal and summary, essential to effective parliamentary participation.

Exercise 5—Handling Amendments.   Because the amendment procedure is one of the most useful in parliamentary practice, and because it is one that students find entertaining and intriguing, several practice sessions can well be devoted to it. The first of these should be arbitrarily limited to primary amendments, and aimed at clarifying the basic amendment process and the principles for determining what is germane as these things are outlined in Lesson 6.

Exercise 6—Handling Amendments (Continued).   More sophisticated exercises in the amendment procedure can permit the use first of secondary amendments and later hostile ones, the acceptance of amendments by the proposer, and amendments by creating blanks as these are explained in Lesson 6.

Exercise 7—Using Subsidiary Motions.   After the study of subsidiary motions has been completed with Lesson 9, exercises in the use of postponing indefinitely, referring to a committee, postponing to a certain time, and tabling can profitably be held. Students will alternate in the chair to develop skill and confidence in handling the special problems these procedures can create in typical parliamentary practice.

Exercise 8—Forming an Organization.   After Lesson 14 has been completed it will be useful and genuinely interesting to have the class organize itself into a formally constituted club or society. The first exercise in this connection can be the first organizational meeting of this group as explained in Lesson 25.

Exercise 9—Drafting a Constitution.   If Exercise 8 is used, an auxiliary exercise in connection with it might well be the drafting of a constitution by each member of the class. This might be the proposed constitution for the class organization, with each member using his own version with its special features and details.

Exercise 10—Adopting a Constitution.   If Exercises 8 and 9 are used, then the next exercise may well be the second organizational meeting of the class, in which the constitution would be adopted and permanent officers elected.

Exercise 11—Using the Emergency Procedures. When the class has been formally organized, it can significantly and practically engage in exercises involving special emergency procedures, the motions to close and limit debate, and to revote and undo business.

Exercise 12—Review Practice. Continuing sessions of the duly constituted class group, following the regular order of business in which all of the motions and procedures occur, can profitably be used. These will serve to consolidate the knowledge and develop the skill of the class, both as members and as officers, particularly if different members of the class are permitted to serve as chairman and secretary.

Bibliography

FOR THOSE who would like to broaden their knowledge in parliamentary procedure, the following brief bibliography is furnished, with no apologies for its brevity. On the whole, not much has been written, and since Robert, very little, that is new. For the past twenty years the author has attempted to collect everything published, as well as everything that can be found from old bookstores and book collectors. These do not quite fill a five-foot bookshelf. It is true also that skill both in participating in meetings and in presiding will be gained more from the practice of the procedures that are detailed in this book than from delving into the complexities of the rare and unusual problems in which the more detailed treatises inevitably become involved.

On these assumptions this list is furnished. It contains 1. several basic and authoritative references on the rules; 2. several textbook-like approaches to parliamentary practices; 3. several books of historical interest; 4. several of international interest; 5. one on the legal aspects of parliamentary procedure of particular interest to future lawyers, legislators, congressmen, and senators, and finally, 6. a periodical published by parliamentarians devoted to procedural problems.

Robert, Henry M. *Rules of Order Revised*, Seventy-fifth Anniversary Edition. Chicago: Scott, Foresman and Co., 1951.
This is the basic authority and the standard code of rules by which most American organizations are constitutionally required to operate.

Sturgis, Alice F. *Standard Code of Parliamentary Procedure*. New York: McGraw-Hill Book Co., 1950.

This is another code of the rules intended for the same purpose as Robert's; it has been constitutionally adopted by some American associations on the ground that it is more readable and understandable.

Robert, Henry M. *Parliamentary Practice*. New York: Appleton-Century Crofts, Inc., 1921.

This is a book illustrating and explaining the simpler rules and customs of deliberative assemblies, written by Robert for beginners forty-five years and half a million copies after the first publication of the *Rules*.

Sturgis, Alice F. and Alta B. Hall. *Textbook on Parliamentary Law*. New York: Macmillan Company, 1923.

The pioneering textbook in parliamentary procedure with twenty-three lessons, exercises, model forms, and detailed charts.

Sturgis, Alice F. *Learning Parliamentary Procedure*. New York: McGraw-Hill Book Co., 1953.

A more extensive presentation of parliamentary practice, including materials on committees, conferences, and conventions, the history of procedure, and practice projects.

Jefferson, Thomas. *Manual of Parliamentary Practice*. Philadelphia: Hogan and Thompson, 1848.

This is the work composed originally by Jefferson for the use of the Senate of the United States. It is a collector's item, but still to be found in some libraries. Its content is readily available in the *Senate Manual* listed as the next item.

Harrison, G. F. and John P. Goder. *Senate Manual*. Washington: Government Printing Office, 1959.

Both for its reprinting of Jefferson's rules and for its general interest, students will find the biennially published *Manual* of the Senate or the *Rules* of the House of Representatives worthy of examination.

Bourinot, J. G. *Rules of Order*. Toronto: McClelland and Stewart Ltd., 1924.

An abridgment of this author's larger work as Clerk of the House of Commons, of interest in showing the similarities of procedure in Canada.

More, S. S. *Practice and Procedure of Indian Parliament*. Bombay, India: Thacker and Co., Ltd., 1960.

This book, available in some American libraries, is included as suggestive of a kind that will prove interesting to students concerned with the universality of parliamentary practice. It describes the procedure in Indian parliamentary institutions and compares this with that of Great Britain and the Dominions.

Mason, Paul O. *Manual of Legislative Procedure.* New York: McGraw-Hill Book Co., 1953.

A manual compiled to meet the particular needs of legislative bodies, covering the procedural problems of official public bodies of all kinds. It emphasizes the legal aspects of the rules and will be of special interest to future statesmen and lawyers.

Robert, Henry M. *Parliamentary Law.* New York: Appleton Century Crofts, 1923.

This is Robert's most comprehensive treatise on the rules—588 pages. In addition to a thorough treatment of the method of transacting business in deliberative assemblies, it furnishes the answers to several hundred questions on procedure submitted to Robert during the fifty years following the publication of the *Rules.*

Parliamentary Journal. A scholarly journal published by the American Institute of Parliamentarians, 4453 Beacon Street, Chicago 60640, dedicated to the wider use and improvement of parliamentary procedure, featuring articles on procedure written by professional parliamentarians and other experts in the field of parliamentary practice.

Quick Reference Chart

The Principal Motions

Main Motion			S	D	M
Subsidiary Motions	1.	Postpone indefinitely	S	D	M
	2.	Amend	S	D	M
	3.	Refer to Committee	S	L	M
	4.	Postpone definitely	S	L	M
	5.	Lay on the Table	S	U	M
		Limit Debate	S	L	⅔
		Close Debate	S	U	⅔
		Reconsider	S	D	M
		Repeal	S	D	⅔
		Recess	S	L	M
		Adjourn	S	U	M

Rules

1. Any motion is in order when it makes procedural sense and is made in good faith (see text).
2. Subsidiary motions higher in number are in order when one lower is pending.
3. All these motions require a second.
4. Substantive motions are debatable (D).
5. Procedural motions are undebatable (U).
6. Qualifiable procedural motions permit limited debate (L).
7. Decisions are by majority (M) except those upsetting previous decisions (⅔).

Special Emergency Procedures

Point of Order
Appeal from Chair's Decision
Parliamentary Inquiry

Request for Information
Point of Privilege

Objection to Consideration

These Procedures:

a. are in order at any time,
b. may interrupt when necessary,
c. require no second (except Appeal),
d. are undebatable, and
e. are disposed of immediately without a vote except Appeal (M) and objection (⅔).

Quick Reference Chart

The Principal Motions

Main Motion				S	D	M
Postpone Indefinitely				S	D	N
					D	M

Priority
Subsidiary
Motion

Call Roll						
Close Debate				S	D	⅔
Limit Debate				S	D	N
Recess				S	D	⅔
Recess				S	L	M
Adjourn				S	U	M

Rules

1. Any motion is in order unless it has a procedural amendment to it made in good faith to do it.

2. Subsidiary motions higher in number are in order when that one lower is pending.

3. All these motions remain in demand.

4. Substantive motions are debatable (D).

5. Procedural motions are undebatable (U).

6. Quashable procedural motions permit limited debate (L).

7. Decisions are by majority (M) except those regulating previous decisions (⅔).

Special Emergency Procedures

Point of Order

Appeal from Chair's Decision

Parliamentary Inquiry

Request for Information

Point of Privilege

Objection to Consideration

The so Procedures:

a. are in order at any time,

b. may interrupt when a vote is required,

c. require no second (except Appeal),

d. are undebatable, and

e. are disposed of immediately with no vote except Appeal (M) and objection (⅔).